Twayne's English Authors Series

Sylvia E. Bowman, Editor

INDIANA UNIVERSITY

WITHDRAWN

George Chapman

 60

George Chapman

By CHARLOTTE SPIVACK

University of Massachusetts

Twayne Publishers, Inc.   ::   New York

To Bernard

What I do and what I dream include thee,
As the wine must taste of its own grapes.

Preface

In *George Chapman* it is my aim to provide the reader with a balanced and comprehensive analysis of the works of this poet and playwright. The opening chapter is biographical and includes extracts from letters written by Chapman. The second chapter examines his poetry, both his original verse and the Homeric translations which have, to some extent, conferred on him the fame which he so earnestly sought. Chapters Three and Four deal with the comedies, moving from his early experiments in "humour" comedy to his later attempts in satire and romance. Chapters Five and Six discuss his tragedies, both the heroic epics which portray the careers of defiant Renaissance individualists and the later pieces which offer stoic heroes as tragic models. Chapter Seven surveys contemporary opinions of this significant seventeenth-century writer.

For their kindness in allowing me to use their resources, I wish to thank the librarians of the Folger Shakespeare Library in Washington, D. C.

CHARLOTTE K. SPIVACK

University of Massachusetts

Contents

Chronology

1559 or 1560	George Chapman born in Hitchin, Herfordshire, England.
ca. 1574	Attended Oxford for an uncertain period of time.
ca. 1583	Entered service in the household of Sir Ralph Sadler.
1591	Participated in military action on the Continent.
1594	First extant publication, *The Shadow of Night*.
1595	Published *Ovid's Banquet of Sense*.
ca. 1595–1600	Wrote plays for the Lord Admiral's Men which were performed at Henslowe's Rose Theatre.
1595–96	*The Blind Beggar of Alexandria* performed.
1597	*A Humorous Day's Mirth* performed.
1598	Published a partial translation of Book XVIII of the *Iliad*, called *Achilles Shield*, together with seven books of the *Iliad;* also the four sestiads completing Christopher Marlowe's *Hero and Leander*.
1599	*All Fools* performed. Ceded to a relative all his rights to the family estate.
1600	Arrested for debt to the usurer John Wolfall.
1601–1609	Wrote plays for the Children of the Chapel which were performed at the Blackfriars Theatre.
ca. 1601	*May Day* performed.
ca. 1602	*The Gentleman-Usher* and *Sir Giles Goosecap* performed.
ca. 1604	*Bussy d'Ambois* and *Monsieur d'Olive* performed.
1605	*Eastward Ho* performed. Imprisoned along with Ben Jonson and perhaps John Marston for passages in *Eastward Ho* offensive to James I.
ca. 1605	*The Widow's Tears* performed.
1608	*The Conspiracy and Tragedy of Charles, Duke of Byron* performed. Narrowly escaped imprisonment

	for scenes in *The Conspiracy and Tragedy of Charles, Duke of Byron.*
1609	Published twelve books of the *Iliad;* also *The Tears of Peace.*
1610– ca. 1614	Wrote plays for the Queens Revels Company (a re-organization of the Children of the Chapel) which were performed at the new Whitefriars Theatre.
ca. 1610	*The Revenge of Bussy d'Ambois* performed.
1611	Published entire translation of the *Iliad.*
1612	Death of Prince Henry, his patron, who had promised to subsidize the Homeric translations.
ca. 1612– 1613	Imprisoned for debt. *Caesar and Pompey* performed.
1613	Wrote *Masque of Lincolns Inn and Inner Temple* for the wedding of Princess Elizabeth, daughter of James I.
1614	Published *Andromeda Liberata* to celebrate the marriage of his patron Somerset.
1614– 1615	Published the *Odyssey* in two parts.
1615	Arrest of his patron, Earl of Somerset, for complicity in the Overbury murder.
1616	Published *The Whole Works of Homer,* both epics in a single edition.
1621	Acquitted of the debt charge after long litigation.
ca. 1622	*The Tragedy of Chabot* performed.
ca. 1624	Published the lesser Homerica in *The Crown of Homer's Works.*
1634	Died on May 12; buried with a monument in his honor fashioned by Inigo Jones.

CHAPTER 1

George Chapman, Second Son

BUT for the unknown, devoted friend "I.M.," who commissioned the handsome engraved portrait of George Chapman adorning the 1616 edition of his translations of Homer's epics, the date of the poet's birth would still remain a matter of speculation. The age of fifty-seven thereon recorded tells us that he was born in either 1559 or 1560, and the poet himself has told us where. In "The Tears of Peace" he locates the "fayre Greenes" where he breathed his "native air" in Hitchin, a country town in Herfordshire about thirty miles north of London. Although this is low fen country, "where their mystie ayre is as thick as mould butter and the deaw lies like frothie balme upon the ground," [1] the poet elevated it by providing a lofty hill ("next Hitchins left hand") worthy of entertaining Homer's visiting ghost.

Chapman's family was of honorable stock.[2] His father Thomas was a copyholder, a relatively high social position at that time, and one of the richest men in town. His mother Joan was the daughter of George Nodes, sergeant of the hunting dogs to Henry VIII, and of Margaret Grimeston, a cousin of the historian Edward Grimeston, whose books later furnished George with the plots of his French tragedies. But it was George's misfortune to be a second son: "Tis a poor calling: Though not unlawful, very hard to live on." [3] His elder brother Thomas inherited the family estate along with three hundred pounds, while young George had to be content with one hundred pounds and two silver spoons. Fate seems to have stamped the pattern of Chapman's life in this initial handicap: not only did he suffer lifelong poverty, but he also continually displayed a positive genius for untimely action. By the end of his long career, however, the second son had become a first-rate poet and dramatist, a gentleman and a scholar.

I *Elizabethan Career*

The first specific information about Chapman's adulthood comes from Anthony à Wood,[4] who relates that the young man went to Oxford in 1574, where he excelled in Greek and Latin but faltered in logic and philosophy, an item which critics of his involved sentences have cited knowingly ever since. How long he remained at Oxford is not known, however, and in his epilogue to the Homeric hymns Chapman expressed pride in being self-taught: "he's best Scholler, that through paines and vows; / Made his owne Master onely; all things know's" (11.39–40).

After his sojourn at the university, Chapman spent some time in service in the household of a nobleman, Sir Ralph Sadler. Exactly how long is not known, but an inscription in the Inner Temple Library copy of the *Batrachomyomachia* places him there in 1583, and other sources establish his continuing presence in the same household in 1585. Although the date of his departure from Sadler has not been established, it is known that in 1591–92 Chapman was on the Continent, where he saw military service in the Low Country campaigns. Documentation has confirmed the accuracy of the account given by the poet himself in the "Hymn to Cynthia." With an elaborate simile that has the ring of personal authenticity, he describes in it in detail an attack on "sconce-torne" Nymeghen, an event only briefly described in Grimeston's history of the Netherlands.

Chapman must have returned to England shortly after these campaigns, for the imprint of his first published work, *The Shadow of Night*, is London, 1594. The companion pieces which constitute this allegorical poem have biographical as well as literary significance in the poet's career. Chapman was at that time associated with a group of erudite and individualistic young men—poets, astronomers, mathematicians—led by Sir Walter Raleigh. Devoted to scientific and philosophical speculation, they reputedly dabbled occasionally in the occult. Their esoteric doctrines included hermetic emphasis on the mysterious powers of night as opposed to the banal clarities of day. At this time a rivalry developed between Raleigh's group, which Shakespeare nicknamed "The School of Night," [5] and a faction headed by the Earl of Essex and including Shakespeare. Apparently Shakespeare had an opportunity to read *The Shadow of Night* in manuscript,

for he parodied both the ideas of the school and some of its
members in his play *Love's Labour's Lost.* Chapman then rewrote
parts of the poem, which he published after the play, in which
he counterattacked with a defiant preface addressed to Matthew
Royden, mathematician and fellow member of the "school."

Thomas Nashe joined the literary fracas in 1594 with his mocking "Terrors of the Night," a parody of the five-fold vision related
in Chapman's next poem, *Ovid's Banquet of Sense,* which apparently Nashe had been able to see in manuscript. Nashe's tale
concerns a certain "wise, grave, sensible man" who lived "in the
country some threescore myle off from London" and who was
subjected one night to five visions of temptation. First the devil
bade him fish with silken nets and silver hooks; then lusty sailors
invited him to drink, after which a pageant of stately devils
offered him chests filled with treasure. The last two visions were
more sensuous: first, a troupe of naked virgins encircled his bed;
then, an assembly of matrons, one of whom tried to slip into his
bed. Although rescued from seduction, the tormented gentleman,
weakened by the experience, died two days later.

Although *Ovid's Banquet of Sense,* with its own series of five
tempting visions appealing to each of the five senses, was the last
document to be published in this literary war, Chapman continued his relationship with the Raleigh group for a long time.
In 1596 he wrote a prefatory poem ("De Guiana Carmen
Epicum") for an account of the Raleigh expedition to Guinea,
in which he glorified the heroic enterprise and its daring leader.
In 1598 his fragmentary translation of the *Iliad,* "Achilles Shield,"
included an introductory poem to Thomas Harriot, another member of the Raleigh circle. More important, in 1598 he published
his continuation of Christopher Marlowe's unfinished *Hero and
Leander,* a testimony to the genuine depth of his friendship with
the fellow poet so closely associated with the Raleigh "school"
of bright young skeptics.

Chapman's relationship with Shakespeare at this time remains
a provocative and open question. Could Chapman have been the
"rival poet" of the sonnets? Although the evidence remains—and
is likely to do so—insufficient to support any conclusions about
the relationship, the description of the rival poet in Sonnet 86
suits Chapman more than any other candidate available for the
role. Only Marlowe would be an equally qualified candidate, but

his early death precludes him from consideration. Shakespeare's
reference to "the proud full sail of his great verse" might well
apply to Chapman's style, particularly to the Alexandrines of his
Homeric translations. Even more convincing evidence is the reference to "that affable familiar ghost / Which nightly gulls him
with intelligence." No other poet of the time admitted to such
literal inspiration as Chapman acknowledged from communing
by night with the shade of Homer, an episode he records in "The
Tears of Peace." He even asserted in his dedication to *The
Shadow of Night* that the true poet cannot succeed without inspiration from a "heavenly familiar." Furthermore, that Chapman
had achieved the stature of a genuine rival might well be inferred
from the inclusion of no less than eighty extracts from his poems
in *The English Parnassus*, an anthology edited by Robert Allot
in 1600.

The reputation of Chapman's verses did little to relieve his
financial plight, however; and he complained of the lot of poets
who "live so poore they are of all despised / Theyr gifts, held
down with scorne, should be divined, / And they like Mummers
mask, unknowne, unprised." Even after Chapman began writing
plays for the Lord Admiral's Men (*ca.* 1595), he continued to be
plagued by severe financial pressures. In spite of the fact that he
was paid eight to ten pounds for a play—a good rate for the time
—he found that dependence on a theatrical income resulted only
in humiliating poverty. In 1599, he and his elder brother yielded
their rights to the family estate in exchange for one hundred
twenty pounds: a year later George was in prison for debt. In his
straitened circumstances he had made the desperate mistake of
entering into bonds with a notorious usurer named John Wolfall,
and, although there now seems no question that Chapman was
a victim of fraud, he was arrested for debt on charges brought
against him by the money-lender. In a classic pronouncement,
Wolfall voiced the businessman's indignation about his delinquent
debtor-poet "who at the first beinge a man of verye good parts
and expectation hath sithence verye unadvisedly spent the most
parte of his tyme and his estate in ffruteless and vayne poetry."
Chapman's own caustic protest to a creditor is preserved in the
Dobell manuscript collection of his letters,[6] (one of which may
have been addressed to Wolfall or to some one not known):

Sr—For God's love let me trouble you no more with words nor
epistles. My offer is faire and satisfactorie; a suretie both for the
principall and interest. . . .
>Be but secur'de, youre scriveners aske no more;
>Just dealing men are free though nere so poore.

Here's Poetrie for you. Let me be free then; do not insult, tys vulgar;
you are noble and a lover of virtue: I have labor'd you when others
neglected you; for Mr doctor I have been a factor, of mine own mere
motion, without his desire or desert. Let this be my purgatorie. In
good faith Sr I am busie even for life: let me but live and I will pay
you all: resting all yos: Geo: Ch.

Although not lucrative, Chapman's early career with the Lord
Admiral's Men was nonetheless successful. The earliest play
attributed to him is *The Blind Beggar of Alexandria*, performed
at the Rose Theatre in 1595–96. Extremely popular in its day,
it survives only in mutilated form; since much of its romantic
main plot was lost, what is left intact is merely a series of episodes involving the many disguises of the wily hero for whom it
is named. His next play, *A Humorous Day's Mirth*, was also performed at the Rose, in 1597. It is historically important, for it
antedates Ben Jonson's first "humour" play by over a year. Although Jonson, whose lifelong friendship with Chapman dates
from this period, theorized about the comedy of "humours" and
established the genre with several of his own examples, Chapman deserves credit for inaugurating this highly successful mode
of comedy. After these two plays, Chapman left the Admiral's
Men to join the company of boy actors at St. Paul's. Although
his next play, *All Fools*, was probably performed first at the Rose,
it was taken over at the Blackfriars, where the Children of the
Chapel regularly played.

The remainder of Chapman's dramatic career was to be associated with this coterie theater and with another, the Whitefriars; and these theaters had a select audience that demanded
more sophisticated fare than was usually offered on the boards
of the popular theaters like Shakespeare's Globe.[7] Like the popular stage of any era, the public playhouses of that time con-
formed to national and religious ideals by fostering a bourgeois
moral and political propriety guaranteed not to shock or alienate
the man in the pit. On the other hand, the private theaters,

catering to a more aristocratic audience, were given to satire and cynicism; plots were chosen for their intellectual rather than moral content, and the witty dialogue was often daring in its satirical import. In consequence, clever dramatists courted libel suits continually, and Chapman was no exception: early in his playwriting career he had to answer for topical allusions in *The Old Joiner of Aldgate* (1603), a play based on a contemporary scandal, the text of which is unfortunately lost. On the whole, however, Chapman's plays are outstanding among the fairly brittle repertoire of the private theaters for their high moral tone and gentle humor. Even his conventional master-minding protagonists are gentlemen at heart, manipulating their victims for sport rather than gain.

After the Terentian comedy of *All Fools* (1599), Chapman's *May Day* was staged at the Blackfriars about 1601. The last of his "humour" plays, it adds parody to the comedy of character and situation, with verbal analogues to several currently popular plays. *Sir Giles Goosecap,* a play of uncertain date and unrecorded authorship although the evidence of Chapman's hand is convincing enough, is only in part a "humour" play. The titular figure, along with his companions in the subplot, are conventional "humour" characters; but the main plot involves a romance based on Chaucer's *Troilus and Criseyde.* The split in the mood of the play indicates Chapman's movement away from the "humour" comedy, which he had mastered so well, toward a new comic mode—the romance—in which he was again to play the role of innovator only to lose credit with posterity to successors who exploited the idea more fully. The romantic tragicomedy, the genre so successfully adapted by Beaumont and Fletcher that it has been attributed to them, was actually introduced to the English stage on the eve of the Jacobean period by George Chapman.

His real achievements in the genre follow the experimental *Sir Giles Goosecap. The Gentleman Usher* (1602) and *Monsieur d'Olive* (1604), both romantic tragicomedies, rank high among all of his dramatic compositions. But they differ considerably from each other. Distinct among Chapman's comedies for being written almost entirely in blank verse, *The Gentleman Usher* is also characterized by the music, pageantry, and fantasy typical of the plays intended for the Children of the Chapel. *Monsieur d'Olive*, on the other hand, is written in vigorous, racy prose and has a satirical, realistic subplot contrapuntal to its romantic main plot.

At the close of the Elizabethan period, Chapman was recognized as a leading poet and dramatist. But his successes were ironic. Honored in *The English Parnassus*, acknowledged as successor to Marlowe, perhaps even envied by Shakespeare, the poet was still an impoverished second son, with a law suit over his debts pending ominously and with not a patron in sight. Creator of the comedy of "humours," innovator in the romantic tragicomedy, and the choice of Sir Francis Meres as "among the best in comedy and tragedy," the dramatist was to remain a "second son" in the view of historians of literature: he was slighted in favor of fellow-dramatists who shaped their fame in the molds of his creation.

II *Jacobean Career*

Chapman's Jacobean period had an auspicious beginning. With the accession of James I to the throne, the remarkable young Prince Henry, a sincere patron of the arts though still in his teens, endorsed the poet's Homeric translations with a promise of three hundred pounds and a substantial pension. In 1609 Chapman published the first twelve books of the *Iliad*, dedicated to that beneficent heir to the throne. But the wry fates had not forgotten their second son: in 1612, the youthful prince, only eighteen, died of a mysterious disease, Hungarian fever, which ironically only Chapman has identified for posterity. Genuinely moved by the premature death of his promising patron, the poet composed an elegy, "The Epicedium," in which he idealized the young man as a worthy descendant of the great Elizabethan tradition, possessor of heroic virtue like the great adventurers of those golden days. Nobly, Chapman dedicated the poem to an obscure friend, a Henry Jones; tactlessly, he praised the dead son too much at the expense of the living father. The king never fulfilled Henry's deathbed promise of sustained patronage, a dismal fact of which Chapman bitterly complained ever after. He addressed desperate pleas for justice both to the king and to members of the privy council. He petitioned the Earl of Northampton, lord privy seal:

Beseeching yoe good lo^p to vouchsafe the reading of the annext peti-
tion, and to take notice of my enforced suite therein contained; The
ground thereof being a due debt (the promise of a Prince vouched
on his deathbed) growing from a serious and valuable cause (two
yeares studious writinge impos'd by his highness upon a poore man,
whose Pen is his Plough, and the sole meanes of his maintenance) that
yoe Lo^p, being a most competent Judge of my paines in this kinde;
may please out of your noble inclination to learning, to countenance
my constrained motion, made for no money; but only for some poore
Coppiehold of the Princes land, of 40 £ Rent, if any such I can find.
Nor needes yoe Lo^p doubt giving President to any, no one being able,
of this nature, to allege the like service; none but myself having done
Homer; which will sufficiently distinguish it from any other: for if
what Virgile divinely affirmes be true, that easier it is to gaine the
Club from Hercules than a verse from Homer (intending so to gaine
and manadge it that we make it our owne) I hope few els can plead to
the Prince so difficult a service.

But Chapman remained a poet without a patron. Meanwhile,
fresh problems awaited him in his theatrical career. With his
dramatic reputation well established, Chapman moved into the
Jacobean period with his two last comedies, *The Widow's Tears,*
a bitter play with tragic overtones, and *Eastward Ho,* a realistic
piece about London life written in collaboration with his friends
Marston and Jonson. Although the latter play was immensely
popular, its gay irreverence toward the Scots and its mocking
allusions to the recent Virginia expeditions promptly threw two
of its three authors into jail. Marston somehow escaped both the
wrath of the king and the hands of his officers. For a tense time,
rumor threatened that offenders Jonson and Chapman were to
have their noses slit, but the playwrights were released after
Chapman's epistolary petitions to the king and other dignitaries.
He mustered his rhetorical resources to assert his innocence: "I
doubt not but the Tempest that hath dryven me into this wrack-
full harbor will cleere with my Innocence; And withall the most
sorrow inflicting wrath of his Excellent Majestie, which to my
most humble and zealous affection is so much the more stormy,
by how much some of my obscured laboures have striv'd to aspire
instead therof his illustrate favoure: And shall not be the least
honor to his most Royall vertues."
And he somewhat ungenerously disclaimed the offending lines,

perhaps in the assurance that Marston was safely out of reach: "Vouchsafe most Excellent Soveraigne to take mercifull notice of the submissive and amendfull sorrowes of your two most humble and prostrated subjects for your highnes displeasure: Geo: Chapman and Ben Jhonson; whose chief offences are but two clawses, and both of them not our owne; much less the unnaturall issue of our offenceles intents." In any event, the scandal seemingly assured the success of the play, which appeared in three editions in 1605 and had a long tenure on the stage.

Chapman abandoned comedy after *The Widow's Tears*, which was probably written shortly after *Eastward Ho*. Most of his Jacobean career as a dramatist was devoted to tragedy. As a tragedian, he produced a total of six plays, five of which were based on contemporaneous French history. His first and best-known was the melodramatic *Bussy D'Ambois*, probably written about 1604 and played by the Children of St. Paul's. In 1610 it was revised by Nathan Field, an actor and a close friend of Chapman, for a Whitefriars performance; and it was revived during the Restoration. Based on the adventures of a colorful French courtier, the play displays the sensationalism and the impassioned rhetoric so popular at that time. Its sequel (but not the next play that Chapman wrote), *The Revenge of Bussy*, is a very different kind of drama. In many ways a theatrically weak play, it featured an unconventional avenger-hero, Clermont, who is too much of a gentleman and a scholar to stoop to the vengeful duties required of him by his brother Bussy's ghost.

Composed between *Bussy* and its sequel was the two-part tragic drama, *The Conspiracy and Tragedy of Byron*. A contemporary reference to this play fixes its date exactly in the spring of 1608: the French ambassador wrote a letter complaining about a performance of this play, boasting that he had effected the arrest of the three principal players although the author had escaped.[8] The particularly offensive scene, which had outraged the ambassador, was one in which the French queen boxes the ears of the king's mistress. Other scenes were also deleted by the censor, however, so that the fourth act of *The Conspiracy* has virtually disappeared; and the first two acts of *The Tragedy* are also drastically expunged. Chapman complained bitterly in the Dedication of these "poor dismembered poems," but he had barely escaped another imprisonment. He was, in fact, forced to

take shelter with the Duke of Lennox, to whom he addressed a
letter of gratitude:

Sr: Not wearie of my Shelter, but uncertaine why the forme of the
cloude still hovers over me, when the matter is disperst, I write to
intreate your resolution; And all this tyme have not in this sort visited
you, for feare I should seeme to give spurrs to your free disposition;
But now (least imagininge me hotter of my libertie than I am, you
should thinke me unhowsd, and not to have presented you with my
first thankfull Apparence) I thought good to send out this dove; And
thoughe I am put, by the Austeritie of the offended tyme to this little
pacience, yet can I not be so thanklesslye jelouse of the knowing
judgment from whence your actions proceede to retaine any thought of
youre favours Repentance; or neglect of their extension in the safe
retreat: when your daungerous charge for me was so resolute and
worthie.

But toward the licenser for the press, he directed an angry scorn
worthy of the fiery temperament of his character Byron. In an
acid letter, Chapman recalled the abused manuscript:

Whosoever it were that first plaied the bitter Informer before the
frenche Ambassador for a matter so far from offence; And of so much
honor for his maister as those two partes contained, perform'd it with
the Gall of a Wulff, and not of a man: . . . But how safely soever
Illiterate Aucthoritie setts up his Bristles against Poverty, methinks
yours (being accompanied with learning) should rebate the pointes
of them, and soften the fiercenes of those rude manners; you know
Sr. They are sparkes of the lowest fier in Nature that fly out uppon
weaknes with every puffe of Power; I desir not you should drenche
your hand in the least daunger for mee: And therefore (with entreatie
of my Papers returne) I cease ever to trouble you.

The last of Chapman's tragedies dealing with French history
was *Chabot*, which, not licensed until 1635, was probably written
considerably earlier. Although the plot was ostensibly based on
the episode of a French admiral's trial recorded in Etienne Pasquier's *Les Recherches de la France*, it is strikingly parallel to
the English trial of the Earl of Somerset, Chapman's patron. The
implications of this analogy grow out of the long, episodic relationship between the poet and his unstable patron, Robert Carr,
later Earl of Somerset. With unfaltering personal fidelity, Chap-

man defended the amiable but luckless Carr in the two major crises of his life and remained loyal to him during the several years of the latter's imprisonment in the Tower. The first crisis concerned Carr's marriage to Frances Howard, divorced wife of the Earl of Essex. While acting as secretary to King James, Carr had begun an intrigue with Lady Frances, the Countess of Essex, as a result of which she asked for an annulment of her marriage on the grounds that her elderly husband was impotent.

After a prolonged, scandalous court battle, the lady won her freedom; but her consequent marriage with Carr achieved a notoriety that was only worsened by Chapman's tactless celebration of the event in *Andromeda Liberata*. Astonishing to no one but the poet was the general interpretation of the "rock" from which Andromeda was liberated as the person of Essex. To still the subsequent accusations of slander, Chapman was forced to follow the poem with another, that was prefaced by a prose statement and entitled, *A Free and Offenceles Justification: Of a lately publish't and most maliciously misinterpreted Poeme; Entituled, Andromeda Liberata*. In his preface he explained his choice of myth: "The Nuptials of *Perseus* and *Andromeda*, an innocent and spotlesse virgine, rescu'd from the polluted throate of a monster; which I in this place applied to the sauage multitude; peruerting her most lawfully-sought propagation, both of blood and blessing, to their owne most lawlesse and lasciuious intentions: from which in all right she was legally and formally deliuered."

But Chapman's arch opportunity to defend his patron came when the triumphant bridegroom later discovered that his arduously won bride was a murderess. As subsequent events established, Lady Frances had hired a druggist's boy to administer a poisonous injection to Thomas Overbury, the character-writer, who was imprisoned in the Tower of London on apparently fraudulent charges. The well-known writer had been at one time a close friend of Carr but had incurred the anger of Lady Frances, who considered him an enemy. Although Carr's career at court flourished for a time after the marriage and he became Earl of Somerset, when the sordid facts of the Overbury case came to light, the couple were immediately implicated and disgraced. They were tried at court with Sir Francis Bacon acting as prosecutor, and, although Robert pleaded innocent, he was sentenced, as was his wife, who confessed her guilt. Eventually both were pardoned, but those who were convinced of Robert's innocence also felt that both Bacon and the King, who had acquired a new favorite jealous of the popular Somerset, had unjustly urged his conviction because of personal malice. This time Chapman's defense was formulated in better taste: *Chabot*, written after Somerset's fall from power, was at least in part a plea for mercy on behalf of his former patron.[9] The dramatic exposure of those false accusations which at first overwhelmed the loyal, frank hero, Chabot, but later involved the prosecutors in infamous perversions of truth and justice, undoubtedly reflected Chapman's faith in the integrity of his patron and his suspicion of calumny on the part of Bacon. After Somerset's release from the Tower in 1622, the poet dedicated *The Crown of Homer's Works* to him.

Chapman's least reputed tragedy, and perhaps his last, was *Caesar and Pompey*, Although for a long time accepted as his last play, this Roman tragedy has, however, come to be regarded in some recent scholarly opinion as an early production, one close to *Bussy* in time of composition.[10] With typical didactic intent, it embodies the explicit proposition that only the just man is free. If this play did follow the French tragedies, *Caesar and Pompey* completed the dramatic career of George Chapman. Although actively writing and translating during his last decades, to the best of our knowledge he abandoned the theater. Whether or not he continued to write masques after the highly successful *Masque of the Inner Temple*, written in 1613 to celebrate the wedding of Princess Elizabeth, remains an open question. Jonson's encomium to Chapman as his only equal as a writer of masques piques the scholar's curiosity, but history unhappily has left no evidence of such works.[11]

Numerous occasional verses written during Chapman's Jacobean career reflect the poet's continually frustrated search for a patron. The long, allegorical poem *Euthymiae Raptus, or The Tears of Peace*, which appeared in 1609, had been dedicated to the ill-fated Prince Henry; and the important elegy for the Prince was surprisingly dedicated to Henry Jones, a friend about whom nothing is known beyond the fact that he possessed an autographed copy of Chapman's *Iliad*. Two of his dedications to Edward Phillips, a member of the Prince's household, suggest an oblique request for extra-princely patronage: the *Masque of the Inner Temple* was dedicated to him as was the volume of translations called *Petrarch's Penitentiall Psalms, etc.* Apologetic for the "slendernesse of the volume," Chapman professed reserving his main energies for the greater task of translation, "my thrice humble dutie to his Highnesse." But the dedicatory sonnets appended to those neglected translations chiefly suggest the desperate effort to acquire patronage. Several are to members of the Sidney-Pembroke family, always noted for their generosity to men of letters; one is to Shakespeare's patron, the Earl of Southampton; several others express gratitude for past favors. Only one is known to have been successful, that addressed to the Viscount Rochester, who eventually became the unfortunate Earl of Somerset.

The occasional verses embodying requests are no more numerous than those containing tributes to his contemporaries in the theater. More than conventionally generous in his praises, Chapman had a reputation for encouraging other playwrights and actors in this era of hard struggle for fame and survival. He complimented his old friend Ben Jonson on *Volpone* and *Sejanus;* his actor-protégé Nathan Field for his *Weather-Cocke Woman;* John Fletcher for his pastoral pieces, both poems and plays. And he did not neglect the non-dramatic arts: he penned commendatory verses to the composers William Byrd, John Bull, and Orlando Gibbons, and to Edward Grimeston as translator.

In contrast to the mood of genuine magnanimity characterizing these poems is the late manuscript blast at his old friend, Ben Jonson. It is much to Chapman's credit, however, that he never attempted to publish his satirical diatribe during his lifetime; Jonson would scarcely have suppressed his anger so successfully. Entitled "An Invective . . . against Mr. Ben Jonson," the poem may reflect Chapman's decision to take sides with Inigo Jones,[12] mutual friend and collaborator of the two poets, who had at that time broken off his friendship with Jonson after mounting tension and disagreement between them.

Although Chapman had struggled all his life under a perverse star that inflicted poverty and imprisonment and spirited away his most promising patrons, he at last achieved "the work that I was born to do." The *Iliad* was printed in 1611, the *Odyssey* in two parts in 1614–15, and the *Crown of Homer's Works,* including the *Batrachomyomachia, Hymns,* and *Epigrams,* in 1624. The last collection was printed in a strikingly handsome volume, one which quite outshone even the impressive books which contained the epics. The elaborate title page showed a heavily bearded and laurel-crowned Homer placed above an equally bearded but cloud-haloed Chapman, and printed on the page was the motto *Conscium evasi diem.* The poet who had complained all his life of his failure to be appreciated—or even understood—by the ignorant majority of readers must have felt finally gratified by the publication of these lavish texts. The fates had at last relaxed their harassment of the second son. When Chapman died on May 12, 1634, Inigo Jones fashioned in his honor a Roman style monument that would have pleased his Classic soul because of the elegant simplicity of its appearance and its inscription: "Georgis Chapmanus, poeta Homericus, Philosophers verus, (etsi Christianus poeta)."

III *Portrait of a Poet*

Such is the brief account of the long life of George Chapman. Many lacunae remain: it is not known whether he ever married; of his activities before the age of thirty, when he published his first poetry, only a few fragmentary details survive; and his whereabouts after his theatrical career until the time of his death remain the object of speculation. The relative paucity of biographical information about Chapman is balanced, however, by a plenitude of personal allusions from which one can infer the character of the man. It is easier, therefore, to draw a moral portrait of Chapman than to sketch a biographical profile. The poet revealed much about himself in his letters, of which several are extant, and in the prefaces and dedicatory epistles attached to his works. Like blunt Ben Jonson, he never hesitated to declare, unflinchingly, his own point of view—however unconventional. In addition to his own testimony, several verbal portraits of Chapman by his contemporaries offer both direct description and indirect caricature.

The character of Bellamont in *Northward Ho* by Thomas Dekker and John Webster is generally acknowledged as a good-natured parody of Chapman. In this comedy of cuckoldry and intrigue, the figure of the aged poet is at once that of a dignified, aloof observer of amorous adventure and that of an innocent victim of a most undignified plot to involve him with a prostitute. In the scene in which Bellamont is confronted with the prostitute

Doll, disguised as a lady who requests of him "12 posies for a cheese trencher," the poet "that hath made 500 fools" does not permit himself to be made one. He parries her quips and departs in a burst of eloquent indignation, leaving Doll melancholy and smitten: "I will instantly go and make myself drunk till I have lost my memory. Love a scoffing poet!"

The scene which most clearly identifies Bellamont as Chapman occurs in the beginning of the fourth act. It is night, and the poet, in his nightcap, is scribbling by candlelight; he is so absorbed in his writing that he will not be disturbed "though a sharer bawl." He describes himself as a "poor, unpreferred scholar"; and, when a swaggering intruder interrupts his concentration, he regales him with plots and persons out of his French tragedies, with specific references to the "Duke of Byron" and to the "Admiral of France." Later in the play Bellamont and his friends visit Bedlam, where his assertion of the "divine furor" is taken literally; and he is confined as a madman. But again he emerges triumphant from the prank which has victimized him. It is not he who loses the bet which initiated the series of escapades in the play, but rather he has the last words on the subject: "Who pays for the northern voyage now, lads?" This interesting and by no means uncomplimentary portrayal is so accurate in most of its details that it may well be valid as well in the one completely unsubstantiated item—the existence of Bellamont's scapegrace son, Phillip.[13]

At least a speculative basis exists for assuming the authenticity of the episode involving a prostitute. In one collection of letters, including several signed by Chapman, one unsigned epistle is addressed to a female of that vocation:

You demaunde what you shall doe, the woman on the banke syde can better resolve you. Live under your owne starres. Some happie influence no doubt attends you; If you prosper I will never dispaire. Onlie thus much, I think that all that love which is built on your beautie will ruine when the foundation fayles; for my selfe I speake it to the face of heaven, that I once loved you willinge; I should have esteemed my selfe happie if I might have made you so: Blessed if I might have enjoyed you so: But I finde a Page or a gentleman-usher may with a good face and omnipotent golde, make an honest woman a whoore, but to make a whoore an honest woman is beyond the labours of Hercules; but let experience teach you youre error. I envie not him that shall possess you. If you have wronged me let your owne inconstancye punish it selfe; for I cannot wish you worsse then to be what you are.

Chapman was apparently a proud and aloof man; he was quick to take offense, querulous, scornful of the vulgar multitude (which included just about everyone at one time or another), and heavy-handed though impeccably sincere in his personal pronouncements. Lacking both the grace of a courtier and the sophistication of many of his fellow dramatists, he evokes rather the double image of the cloistered, naïve pedant on the one hand, and of the obstreperous old soldier on the other. Militant in his convictions and scholarly in his aggressions, he was half Bussy, half Clermont—or, as Chapman would probably have preferred, half Achilles, half Odysseus.

Chapman's later years, after his disappearance from the theatrical world of London, remain a mystery. On the one hand, Anthony à Wood's description of the elderly figure as "reverend, religious, and sober," communicates the austere temperament of this intense, dedicated man and the respect it commanded from his contemporaries. But, on the other, a poignant letter in the Dobell collection suggests an impoverished old age of humility and frustration. In an appeal to a friend or patron, Chapman wrote:

Right Worthy, let me once again entreate & humblie beseche you to consyder and pittie the hard extremes of a poore olde man, & let him not perishe in your defalt, whose better yeeres was then best spent, when he toke pleasure in pleasuring others. . . . Conceyt what a tyrant is auncyent povertie: O, it is a devill & furye of hell; It breakes all lawes, respects no persons, nor feares no perilles. It observes neither reason, sence, humanitie, scilence, nor secresie. . . . If you thinke me to bolde to importune you thus, it is not my custome, but my want that compelles me: for while I had meanes to relieve my selfe, I made no demaundes nor pleaded no wants.

In spite of some real moments of indigence, however, Chapman apparently made not merely a reputation but also a profit as a writer of masques during his later years. Again a letter sheds speculative light, if not actual illumination. Although not definitely established as Chapman's, it recalls his style in its haggling demand for as much money as the mere "snipperados" are paid for their menial contributions to the performance; moreover, it echoes that of Capriccio, a figure in the Lincoln's Inn masque: "How hard this world is to a man of wit! He must eat through main rocks for his food, or fast."

And though valuing my labours, *ex condigno*, they might be thought alreadie to have receyved sufficient rewarde; yet considering that others of meaner employment were most liberally dealt with; I may, *ex congruo*, challenge a part in youre equall distribution; And seeing players, dancers, and painters were rewarded out of your full bounty; I think it hard that I (the wryter, and in part inventour) should be put with taylors and Shoomakers, and such snipperados, to be paid by a bill of particulars, what such or such a piece should be pris'd at; or whether the whole summe might amount to above ten pounds or no.

The specter of poverty which haunted Chapman's second-son status throughout his long life serves but to sharpen the outlines of his proud intellect and passionate soul. Loved by such men as John Fletcher and Nathan Field, honored by many of the literary commentators of his time, and emulated by the young dramatists who looked to him for guidance and received it in generous measure, Chapman was obviously a successful man as well as poet; he fulfilled his own humanistic credo: "Learning the art is of good life; those who live not good lives are not learned men." [14]

CHAPTER 2

The Beyond-Sea Muse

CHAPMAN was many poets in one. Although the diverse nature of his poetic output makes it virtually impossible to identify him exclusively with any one school of poetry, his wholehearted subscription to several current modes renders it equally impossible to avoid classification altogether. As a poet, Chapman was by no means an unconventional individualist; he was instead a tireless, skilled experimenter who achieved at different times a mastery of several traditions of poetry. He turned early to the metaphysical style of "conceited" verse; he later became a neo-Classic satirist wielding the heroic couplet; he often reverted to a decidedly medieval allegorical form; and he ultimately settled down to the scholarly art of Homeric translation with a perverse penchant for the archaic fourteener, the long medieval line of fourteen syllables. Along with this versatility of technique, Chapman also developed a fairly comprehensive poetics, that includes points of view about the source and function of poetry, the philosophical implications of technique, and the art of translation. Ultimately, his poetics, like his metaphysics, was Platonic; and, although dispersed throughout his poems, prefatory verses, and epistles, these pronouncements on the art of poesy are unified by the governing principle of Platonic dualism.

I Chapman's Poetics

Bellamont, the good-natured caricature of Chapman in *Northward Ho*, boasts that he is "haunted with a fury" and admits to feeling at home in Bedlam "for your best poets, indeed, are mad for the most part." This feature of the portrait is drawn from one of Chapman's central and notorious convictions: the theory of the divine furor. Plato explains the theory in the *Phaedrus* and in the *Ion*, knowledge of which the poet probably acquired indirectly through Ficino's *Epitomae:*

Phaedrus: The third kind is the madness of those who are possessed by the Muses; which taking hold of a delicate and virgin soul, and there inspiring frenzy, awakens lyrical and all other numbers; with those adorning the myriad actions of ancient heroes for the instruction of posterity. But he who, having no touch of the Muses' madness in his soul, comes to the door and thinks that he will get into the temple by the help of art—he, I say, and his poetry are not admitted; the sane man disappears and is nowhere when he enters into rivalry with the madman. (*Phaedrus*)
Socrates: For all good poets, epic as well as lyric, compose their beautiful poems not by art, but because they are inspired and possessed. And as the Corybantian revellers when they dance are not in their right mind when they are composing their beautiful strains: but when falling under the power of music and meter they are inspired and possessed; . . . beautiful poems are not human, or the work of man, but divine and the work of God. (*Ion*)[1]

Aware of the fine line dividing this divine furor from demonic madness, Chapman carefully distinguished between the "twofold nature" of this "alienation of soul," only one of which results in poetry; the other ends in Bedlam. In an epistle to Somerset, appended to the *Odyssey*, he explained: "One *Insania*, a disease of the mind, and a meere madnesse, by which the infected is thrust beneath all the degrees of humanitie. . . . the other is *diuinis furor;* by which the sound and diuinely healthfull *supra hominis naturam erigitur*, & *in Deum transit*," (II. 77–84). He then cites Homer as the supreme example of the divine fury.

As did Milton in his epics, Chapman also equated the notion of inspiration with Christian grace. In the epistle dedicatory to the *Homeric Hymns*, he adds the following lines to a quotation from Ficino on the subject:

> Yet th'ancient learn'd, heat with celestiall fire,
> Affirmes her flames so sacred and entire;
> That, not without Gods greatest grace she can
> Fall in the wid'st Capacitie of Man. (ll. 132–35)

Chapman received his own divine inspiration directly from that "most wise and divine" poetic exemplar of it: he tells the reader in his Induction to "The Tears of Peace" that he was visited by the shade of Homer. While rapt in meditation, Chapman sud-

denly perceived a light breaking through the shadows; and in
this mystical meeting Homer imparted his true meaning to his
chosen translator:

> . . . and, after it, the sight
> Of a most graue, and goodly person shinde;
> With eys turned vpwards, & was outward, blind;
> But, inward; past, and future things, he sawe;
> And was to both, and present times, their lawe.
> His sacred bosome was so full of fire,
> That t'was transparent; and made him expire
> His breath in flames, that did instruct (me thought)
> And (as my soule were then at full) they wrought. (ll. 34–42)

In his conception of the function of poetry, Chapman assumed
a humanistic position, ultimately Platonic. He exalted the moral
purpose of poetry and regarded the task of the poet as a Promethean undertaking. He expounded this interpretation of the myth
literally in *The Shadow of Night*. As Prometheus made man, with
fire fetched from heaven,

> Therefore Promethean Poets with the coles
> Of their most geniale, more-then-humane soules
> In liuing verse, created men like these,
> With shapes of Centaurs, Harpies, Lapithes,
> That they in prime of erudition,
> When almost sauage vulgar men were growne,
> Seeing them selues in those Pierean founts,
> Might mend their mindes, asham'd of such accounts. (ll. 131–38)

In the higher spiritual sense of the myth, however, Promethean
poets strike fire in the minds and souls of living men. As he asserts in the epistle dedicatory to the *Iliad:* ". . . her Promethean
facultie / Can create men, and make euen death to liue; / For
which she should liue honor'd" (ll. 137–39). For this reason
poetry, currently suffering popular neglect, should be honored
above all the arts. Kings should help her in order that she might
raise their spirits toward virtue: "Who raise her, raise themselues:
and he sits sure, / Whom her wing'd hand aduanceth; since on it
/ Eternitie doth (crowning Vertue) sit" (ll. 147–49). Poetic
tragedy, also fallen into decadence, had a specific Promethean

power that was well recognized in ancient Greece but not sufficiently acknowledged in contemporary times:

> Muses that Fames loose feathers beautifie,
> And such as scorne to tread the Theater,
> As ignorant: the seede of memorie
> Haue most inspirde, and showne theyr glories there
> To noblest wits, and men of highest doome,
> That for the kingly Lawrell bent affayre;
> The Theaters of *Athens* and of *Rome*
> Haue beene the Crownes, and not the base empayre.
>   (*A Coronet, Sonnet* 10, ll. 1–8)

As indicated in his dedication to *The Revenge of Bussy d'Ambois,* Chapman took pride in his own tragedies as vehicles of
moral truth: "material instruction, elegant and sententious excita-
tion to virtue, and deflection from her contrary, being the soul,
limbs, and limits of an autentical tragedy."

Chapman regarded the art of poetry from the viewpoint of
philosophical as well as moral didacticism. He equated literature
with allegory, an approach which derived ultimately from his
double view of reality as matter and spirit. A confirmed Platonist
in his idealism, he expected poetry to postulate the tangible
world as symbolic of the spiritual: poetry is the pulse of the soul.
He repeatedly justified his own use of allegory, as in the address
to Somerset appended to the *Odyssey:*

Nor is this all-comprising *Poesie,* phantastique, or meere fictiue; but
the most material, and doctrinall illations of *Truth;* both for all manly
information of Manners in the yong; all prescription of Iustice, and
euen Christian pietie, in the most graue and high-gouerned. To illustrate both which, in both kinds, with all height of expression, the Poet
creates both a Bodie and a Soule in them. Wherein, if the Bodie
(being the letter, or historie) seemes fictiue, and beyond Possibilitie
to bring into Act: the sence then and Allegorie (which is the soule)
is to be sought: which intends a more eminent expressure of *Vertue,*
for her louelinesse; and of *Vice* for her uglinesse, in their seuerall
effects; going beyond the life, then any Art within life, can possibly
delineate. (ll. 43–55)

Well aware of the obscurity inherent in the allegorical method,
he was by no means reluctant to accept it; indeed, he embraced

it with enthusiasm and confirmed it through the authority of the
past:

As *Learning*, hath delighted from her Cradle, to hide her selfe from
the base and prophane *Vulgare*, her ancient Enemy; under diuers
vailes of *Hieroglyphickes*, Fables, and the like; So both she pleased
her selfe with no disguise more; then in misteries and allegoricall fic-
tions of *Poesie*. . . . Yet euer held in high Reuerence and Aucthor-
ity; as supposed to conceale, within the vtter barke (as their Eternities
approue) some sappe of hidden Truth: As either some dimme and
obscure prints of diuinity, and the sacred history; Or the grounds of
naturall, or rules of morall Philosophie, for the recommending of some
vertue, or curing some vice in generall . . . euer (I say) enclosing
within the Rinde, some fruit of knowledge howsoever darkened; and
(by reason of the obscurity) of ambiguous and different construction.
(*Justification . . . of Andromeda Liberata*, ll. 1–5, 10–16, 22–25)

He even defended obscurity (in an epistle to Royden prefixed
to *The Banquet of Sense*) as a way of consecrating his "strange
Poems" to the enlightened few, shielding them from the profane multitude. The obscurity he advocated, however, had to
be inherent in the profundity of the subject and not a mere pedantic appurtenance used to disguise shallow thoughts:

Obscuritie in affection of words, & indigested concets, is pedanticall
and childish; but where it shroudeth it selfe in the hart of his subiect,
vttered with fitnes of figure, and expressiue Epethites; with that darknes wil J still labour to be shadowed: rich Minerals are digd out of
the bowels of the earth, not found in the superficies and dust of it;
charms made of unlerned characters are not consecrate by the Muses
which are diuine artists, but by *Euippes* daughters, that challenged
them with meere nature, whose brests J doubt not had beene well
worthy commendation, if their comparison had not turnd them into
Pyes. (Epistle to Royden, ll. 29–39)

In an epistle directed "To the Understander" and published with
the *Achilles Shield*, Chapman assumed at the start that the "understander" is "not every bodie." If, then, his own style seems
dark and obscure, "it may perhaps seeme darke to ranke riders
or readers that have no more soules than butbolts" (ll. 13–14).
But, in a moment of penetrating candor, he admitted his "farre-
fetcht and, as it were, beyond-sea manner of writing" (ll. 24–25).

The contemporary rhetorical device which best suited Chapman's allegorical bias was the double figure called *Energia* and *Enargia*. This double figure was in effect the linguistic counterpart of his Platonic dualism. George Puttenham's concise definition of the device is useful: "This ornament then is of two sorts, one to satisfie & delight th'eare onely by a goodly outward shew set vpon the matter with words and speaches smothly and tunably running, another by certaine intendments or sence of such wordes & speaches inwardly working a stirre to the mynde. That first qualitie the Greeks called *Enargia,* of this word *argos,* because it geueth a glorious lustre and light. This latter they called *Energia,* or *ergon,* because it wrought with a strong and vertuous operation." [2]

Chapman, who exploited the double figure, recognized in it much more than a merely verbal sophistication. In a provocative statement which touches upon the philosophical implications of the traditional conflict between the naturalistic and the allegorical modes of art, he defended in the Epistle to Royden in *Ovid's Banquet of Sense* that heightening of physical reality necessary to reveal the underlying spiritual reality: "That, *Enargia,* or cleerenes of representation, requird in absolute Poems is not the perspicuous deliuery of a lowe invention; but high, and harty inuention exprest in most significant, and vnaffected phrase: it serues not a skilfull Painters turne, to draw the figure of a face onely to make knowne who it represents; but hee must lymn, giue luster, shaddow, and heightening; which though ignorants will esteeme spic'd, and too curious, yet such as haue the iudiciall perspectiue, will see it hath, motion, spirit, and life" (ll. 15–23). Conscious of the Platonic myth of the cave, he refused merely to hold the mirror up to that world of nature which is but a reflection of reality.

Chapman's approach to the challenging art of translation, like his poetics in general, was based on Platonic idealism. Applying the double view of reality to the subject, he held that the translator should aim to equate his language with the spirit rather than the letter of his original. He had only scorn for the literal translator: "Custome hath made euen th'ablest Agents erre / In these translations; all so much apply / Their paines and cunnings, word for word to render / Their patient Authors," (To the Reader, *Iliad,* ll. 11–14). On the other hand, the genuinely

poetic translator, aware of the higher nature of his text, is guided
by a higher aspiration: "[he should] aspire / As well to reach
the spirit that was spent / In his example; as with arte to pierce /
His Grammar, and etymologie of words" (ll. 23–26).

In discussing the practical as well as the theoretical problems
of translation, Chapman joined ranks with Dante and Du Bellay
in offering a fervent defense of the native vernacular. He not
only considered the English language a worthy vehicle for rendering the beauties of the Greek but rebuked all modern rivals
in a statement more chauvinistic than genuinely critical:

> Our Monosyllables, so kindly fall
> And meete, opposde in rime, as they did kisse:
>   French and Italian, most immetricall;
> Their many syllables, in harsh Collision,
>   Fall as they brake their necks; their bastard Rimes,
> Saluting as they iustl'd in transition,
>   And set our teeth on edge; nor tunes, nor times
> Kept in their falles. (ll. 86–93)

But, if Chapman was momentarily guilty of a narrow nation-
alism, he was quite free from any comparable charge of prejudice
on personal grounds. Well aware of his own flaws as a poet, he
was painfully honest in attempting to enumerate them. And, insofar as valid self-criticism is a criterion of the great critic, Chapman qualified for greatness. His extraordinary frankness was
matched by critical acumen in such a statement as the following,
addressed to the astronomer Harriot, wherein he astutely ana-
lyzed his faults:

> Rich mine of knowledge, ô that my strange muse
> Without this bodies nourishment could vse
> Her zealous faculties, onely t'aspire,
> Instructiue light from your whole Sphere of fire:
> But woe is me, what zeale or power soeuer
> My free soule hath, my body will be neuer
> Able t'attend: neuer shal I enjoy
> Th'end of my happles birth: neuer employ
> That smotherd feruour that in lothed embers,
> Lyes swept from light, and no cleare howre remembers.
> O had your perfect eye Organs to pierce
> Into that Chaos whence this stiffled verse

> By violence breakes: where Gloweworme like doth shine
> In nights of sorrow, this hid soule of mine:
> And how her genuine formes struggle for birth,
> Vnder the clawes of this fowle Panther earth;
> Then vnder all those formes you should discerne
> My loue to you, in my desire to learne. (ll. 31–48)

In this personal statement, as elsewhere in his esthetic theory, the focus is clearly Platonic: the poet seeks to escape his earthly body in order to free, through expression, the Platonic forms perceived in his soul.

Gathered together as a body of poetic doctrine, Chapman's pronouncements bear a striking resemblance to Percy Bysshe Shelley's *Defence of Poetry* (1821). Close to the Elizabethans in many ways, and subject to many of the same influences as Chapman, Shelley also elaborated the Platonic view of poetry as the perception of correspondences between the two planes of reality. But not only the Romantic period offers an analogue since the view of art expressed in William Butler Yeats' "Sailing to Byzantium" parallels the Platonic focus of Chapman's sonnet, "Muses that sing Love's sensual emperie." Yeats recognized that the "paltry" body must decay and die, but the soul will be gathered "into the artifice of eternity." Since only art can communicate the permanent values of the spirit, the poet wishes to be transformed after death not into "any natural thing" but into an artificial bird "of hammered gold and gold enamelling." Just as Yeats rejects "that sensual music," Chapman rejected the "muses that sing loue's sensuall Emperie" in favor of addressing his immortal mistress, Philosophie, and the subject of his verse in her honor is "the maiestie and riches of the mind."

Just as the poetry of Chapman, in all its variety, belongs to the mainstream of the English tradition, so his poetics, although dispersed throughout that poetry, deserves to be recognized as a contribution to the Platonic stream of criticism so central to the history of that tradition.

II *The Metaphysical Poet*

Algernon Charles Swinburne, anticipating the twentieth-century critics,[3] spoke of Chapman's "sensual metaphysics." In a contemporary essay on the metaphysical tradition, T. S. Eliot recognized in Chapman what he called "a direct sensuous appre-

hension of thought, or a recreation of thought into feeling, which is exactly what we find in John Donne." [4] Since then George Williamson, in his study of the Donne tradition,[5] has gone even farther by calling Chapman "the first metaphysical poet." Despite these major critical pronouncements, Chapman has not yet been generally acknowledged for his metaphysical poetry, probably because only a few of his poems can be classified as definitely such. These few poems are of such striking quality, however, as to merit their place in any representative collection of such verse, and their interest is enhanced historically by the fact that they precede those of Donne.[6]

Four of Chapman's major poetic works belong either wholly or partially to the metaphysical school, both for their subject matter and their imagery. *Ovid's Banquet of Sense, A Coronet for My Mistress Philosophy,* the last four sestiads of *Hero and Leander,* and "A Hymn to Our Savior on the Cross" are all concerned with the basic theme of transcending the flesh through the fleshly experience, whether the context is secular, as in the first three, or sacred, as in the last. And all four display the metaphysical conceit, ranging in quality from mere ingenuity to genuine poetic inspiration.

Prefixed to the volume called *Ovid's Banquet of Sense* (which also included the "Coronet" of sonnets as well as some translations) in the form of a letter to Mathew Royden, is a virtual manifesto of the metaphysical approach to poetry. In it the poet declares that these verses are addressed to a select audience: "these searching spirits, whom learning hath made noble, and nobilities sacred." They stress intellectual content over beauty, vigor of expression over form, with an emphasis on "energia, that high and hearty invention exprest in most significant and unaffected phrase." And they are admittedly, even intentionally, difficult: "rich Minerals are digd out of the bowels of the earth, not found in the superficies and dust of it."

Superficially, the *Banquet* is erotic, following the current Ovidian mode, and is akin to Shakespeare's *Venus and Adonis.* In keeping with the amatory vogue, it pictures Ovid celebrating a banquet of all the five senses in the garden of his fictitious mistress Corinna.[7] Although sensual, the sequential vision is actually an enactment of the Platonic ladder of love as celebrated by Baldassare Castiglione, the Italian humanist, and others in the

neo-Platonic school of thought, whose main spokesman was Marsilio Ficino, the Florentine academician. The sensual feast is never completed: instead, it yields to the strictly spiritual dessert of the "Coronet," in which Corinna becomes Philosophy.

The heavily erotic atmosphere of the *Banquet* is continually disturbed by hard intellectual conceits that lift the poem inevitably from the merely physical level to the metaphysical. At times the language achieves a striking metaphysical metaphor, as when the sun is described: "Then did Cyrrhus fill his eyes with fire, / Whose ardor curld the foreheads of the trees, / And made his greene-loue burne in his desire" (Section 2). But at times it deviates unhappily from a brilliant anticipation of Andrew Marvell at his best to a sorry harbinger of Richard Crashaw at his worst: "Loues feete are in his eyes" (Section 14). When Corinna sings with lute upon her thigh, the language is not at all the melodious Elizabethan line of Thomas Campion, but strong intellectual stuff, complete with a marginal gloss from Aristotle:[8]

> O that as Intellects themselves transite
> To eache intellegible quallitie,
> My life might passe into my loues conceit,
> Thus to be form'd in words, her tunes, and breath,
> And with her kysses, sing it selfe to death. (Section 24)

When Ovid, sated with Corinna's song, goes on to enjoy her "sovereign odors," the language abandons the momentarily soft Spenserian tone in favor of sharp scientific imagery:

> And as a Taper burning in the darke
> (As if it threatned euery watchfull eye
> That viewing burns it,) makes that eye his marke,
> And hurls guilt Darts at it continually. (Section 66)

After the banquet of the third sense, Ovid requests a kiss in gratification of the fourth—taste. Corinna's reply is startlingly intellectual:

> Pure love (said she) the purest grace pursues,
> And there is contact, not by application
> Of lips or bodies, but of bodies vertues,

As in our elementale Nation
     Stars by theyr powers, which are theyr heat and light
Do heavenly works, and that which hath probation
     By vertuall contact hath the noblest plight,
Both for the lasting and affinitie
It hath with naturall diuinitie. (Section 92)

But in spite of the coldly Aristotelian prologue, the "Ambrosian kisse" makes him "swoune" with "syrrop to his taste." Then the imagery leaps from syrup to science again:

And as a Pible cast into a Spring,
Wee see a sort of trembling cirkles rise,
One forming other in theyr issuing
Till over all the Fount they circulize,
     So this perpetuall-motion-making kisse,
Is propagate through all my faculties,
     And makes my breast an endlesse Fount of blisse. (Section 99)

Emboldened with the kiss, Ovid then makes a bid for complete gratification of feeling. His philosophical justification of the request recalls "The Ecstasie" of Donne and states the very essence of that poem: "Mindes taint no more with bodies touch or tyre,/ Then bodies nourish with the mindes desire" (Section 103). But the conclusion of the poem is abrupt and ambiguous. Ovid has just touched Corinna's side, making "her start like sparckles from a fire," when he is interrupted by "the view of other dames." Unlike the reader, who at this point feels only frustration, Ovid somehow becomes so euphoric over this unsensational climax that this prim titillation has qualified him to write the *Art of Love*.

The Platonic significance of the unfinished banquet is clear: sensual gratification is a necessary stepping stone to loftier, intellectual love: "But that a fleshlie engine must unfold / A spirituall notion; birth from Princes sprung / Peasants must nurse, free vertue wait on gold" (Section 111). The Platonic ladder is not, however, completed in *Ovid's Banquet* but the ascent must be completed: "My life that in my flesh a Chaos is / Should to a Golden worlde be thus dygested" (Section 25).

The sequence of ten linked sonnets called *A Coronet for My Mistress Philosophy* that follows, rejects the eroticism of the *Ban-*

quet and transcends its "sensual emperie." The interlinking form of the group may have influenced that of Donne's *Coronet of Divine Sonnets,* but it is the striking use of the conceit which establishes this series of poems squarely in the metaphysical tradition. The opening sonnet introduces the subject with such a conceit: "Muses that sing loues sensuall Emperie, / And louers kindling your enraged fires / At *Cupids* bonfires burning in the eye . . ." Then Chapman develops the theme of dualism:

> Blowe with the emptie breath of vaine desires,
> You that prefer the painted Cabinet
>   Before the welthy Iewels it doth store yee,
>   That all your ioyes in dying figures set,
>   And staine the living substance of your glory.
> Abiure those ioyes, abhor their memory,
>   And let my love the honord subiect be
>   Of love, and honors complete historie;
>   Your eyes were neuer yet, let in to see
> The maiestie and riches of the minde,
> But dwell in darknes; for your God is blinde.

Continuing the theme, the second sonnet focuses first on the conflict and then on the resolution of the struggle between flesh and spirit. The violent torments of sensual love "eate your entrails out with exstasies" and "beate your soules in peeces with a pant," but Philosophy is a benevolent mistress: "But my love is the cordiall of soules, / Teaching by passion what perfection is." The simple statement and homely image echo George Herbert.

Love of Philosophy gives "spirit to flesh" and "soule to spirit." Her beauty is absolute: "Her minde (the beame of God) drawes in the fires / Of her chast eyes, from all earths tempting fewell." The poet deems, therefore, that Philosophy shall become his Muse as well as his mistress, and the cycle ends with a sonnet in praise of the tragic theater of Athens and Rome, which were "the Crownes, and not the base empayre."

Chapman's next contribution to metaphysical poetry was his continuation of Marlowe's *Hero and Leander.* The reader of this entire narrative poem is always struck by the difference in tone between Marlowe's opening two sestiads and Chapman's concluding four. And Chapman frequently, although quite unfairly, suffers in the inevitable comparison simply because Marlowe has set the initial tone with his fine "golden" lyricism—liquid, sensuous, and exquisite. What Chapman is doing is obviously very different, yet it is also first-rate poetry. C. S. Lewis[9] regarded these four sestiads as "the work that I was born to do" for the poet, who had himself applied these words to the mission of his Homeric translation.

Chapman's continuation is a tribute to his friendship with Marlowe, with whom he had drunk from the fountain of the Muses, as he tells us. Yet he was well aware that his draft was headier stuff—"more harsh (at least more hard) more graue and hie"—and he proclaimed the metaphysical springs of his own inspiration:

> Then thou most strangely-intellectual fire,
> That proper to my soule hast power t'inspire
> Her burning faculties, and with the wings
> Of thy unspheared flame visitst the springs
> Of spirits immortall; Now, (as swift as Time
> Doth follow Motion) finde th'eternall Clime
> Of his free soule, whose living subject stood
> Up to the chin in the Pyerean flood,
> And drunke to me halfe this Musean storie,
> Inscribing it to deathles Memorie:
> Confer with it, and make my pledge as deepe,
> That neithers draught be consecrate to sleepe. (ll. 183–94)

The moral emphasis of Chapman's continuation is as different as is the language. Whereas Marlowe was concerned mainly with evocation of the lovers' feelings and exaltation of their beauty and their passions, Chapman is, characteristically, concerned with consequences. He does not castigate Leander's sensuality as such but his failure to achieve its spiritualization. Indeed, Leander's metamorphosis was into flesh:

> So to all objects that in compasse came
> Of any sence he had; his sences flame
> Flowd from his parts, with force so virtuall,
> It fir'd with sence things meere insensuall. (ll. 87–90)

Leander failed to formalize his physical relationship through proper ritual; he did not sacramentalize the flesh in marriage. He is made aware of this flaw by the goddess Ceremonie—playing rather the same role as Spenser's Concord—who descends to warn the enamored young man of the need to perform the rites of sanctification.

Meanwhile, when Chapman analyzes the conflict in Hero's mind and the painful contradiction between her inward consciousness of guilt and her outward appearance of innocence, he achieves some of his best poetry. Sometimes he chooses a scientific conceit:

> For as a glasse is an inanimate eie,
> And outward formes imbraceth inwardlie:
> So is the eye an animate glasse that showes
> In-formes without us. (ll. 235–38)

Sometimes he relies on Classic simplicity and artful sound: "Feare fils the chamber, darknes decks the Bride" (l. 154). The third sestiad ends with an echo of Donne: "Rich, fruitfull loue, that doubling selfe estates / Elixir-like contracts, though separates" (ll. 416–17).

Chapman delays the tragic narrative in the fourth sestiad with an allegorical digression: Venus creates the monster Dissimulation (Eronusis) to "wreak her rites abuses." He further prolongs the story by mythically extending the day in the fifth sestiad, where he recounts another wedding. The artificial interruption of the action is more than justified, however, by the quality of the exquisite Epithalamion Teratos. This lyrical gem is written by a Chapman who is neither the metaphysical poet nor the allegorist nor the satirist but the rare Elizabethan lyricist. The metaphysical poet intrudes only once: "Day is abstracted here, / And varied in a triple sphere" (ll. 451–52). The rest of the poem is Edmund Spenser reborn.

Night finally arrives in the sixth sestiad. As Leander plunges to his fateful swim, the doomed lover calls in vain on Neptune who "for haste his forehead hit / Gainst heauens hard Christall" (ll. 197–98). But the tragic death of the lovers does not separate them for long. The poem ends with an Ovidian metamorphosis, as the kind old god of the sea transforms their bodies into "two sweet birds surnam'd th'Athcanthides" (l. 276).

The continuation of *Hero and Leander*, along with *Ovid's*

Banquet of Sense and *A Coronet For His Mistress Philosophy,*
are the major secular manifestations of Chapman's metaphysical
style. His only substantial example of sacred metaphysical verse
is his "Hymn to the Savior on the Cross," itself the only original
poem in a volume of translations from Petrarch and Virgil. F. L.
Schoell long ago noted its affinity with Donne's religious verse, as
Eliot later noted the similarity in the secular verse of the two
poets. Schoell praised Chapman as "metaphysicien et grave dis-
pensateur de 'theological wit.'" [10] To the contemporary reader
the poem is also interesting for its prefiguration of Gerard Manly
Hopkins' metaphysical vein. [11] Two of Chapman's homely metaphors in this sincere hymn suggest Hopkins: "All Churches
powres, thy writ word doth controule; / And mixt it with the
fabulous Alchoran, / A man might boult it out, as floure from
branne" (ll. 60–62). And the striking physiological metaphor
elaborated in these lines:

> All glorie, gratitude, and all auaile,
> Be giuen thy all-deseruing agonie;
> Whose vineger thou Nectar mak'st in me,
> Whose goodnesse freely all my ill turnes good:
> Since thou being crusht, & strained throgh flesh & blood:
> Each nerue and artire needs must tast of thee. (ll. 270–75)

The entire poem is not metaphysical, however; and the uneven-
ness of its diction illustrates the difficulty in categorizing Chapman. Written in heroic couplets, as are many of his verses, it also
serves to illustrate the second poet named George Chapman, the
neo-Classic satirist.

> So in the Church, when controuersie fals,
> It marres her musicke, shakes her batterd wals,
> Grates tender consciences, and weakens faith;
> The bread of life taints, & makes worke for Death;
> Darkens truths light, with her perplext Abysmes,
> And dustlike grinds men into sects and schismes. (ll. 81–86)

The final couplet anticipates the age of Dryden and Pope.

III *The Neo-Classic Satirist*

The neo-Classic Chapman was everything that the metaphysical Chapman was not: the metaphysical poet was strained, obscure, and complex; the neo-Classic poet, polished, urbane, and precise—a very model of incisive clarity. The neo-Classic muse inspired Chapman's most consistently good poetry, and the satiric heroic couplet was his best verbal weapon. The epistles dedicatory to the Homeric translations abound in sharp couplets that rival Pope in dexterity: "Their worst poets, and worst men, their Best subornes, / Like winter Cowes, whose milk runnes to their hornes." And when imagery occurs, it is not devious and tortuous but direct and forthright, as in the following passage which amplifies a single image with complete clarity and sustained vigor:

> But as an Asse, that in a field of weeds
>   Affects a thistle, and falles fiercely to it;
> That pricks, and gals him; yet he feeds, and bleeds;
>   Forbeares a while, and licks; but cannot woo it
> To leaue the sharpnes; when (to wreake his smart)
>   He beates it with his foote; then backward kickes,
> Because the Thistle gald his forward part;
>   Nor leaues till all be eate, for all the prickes;
> Then falles to others with as hote a strife;
>   And in that honourable warre doth waste
> The tall heate of his stomacke, and his life;
>   So, in this world of weeds, you worldlings taste
> Your most-lou'd dainties; with such warre, buy peace;
>   Hunger for torments; vertue kicke for vice;
> Cares, for your states, do with your states increase:
>   And though ye dreame ye feast in Paradise,
> Yet Reasons Day-light, shewes ye at your meate
>   Asses at Thistles, bleeding as ye eate. ("To the Reader,"
>   *Iliad*, ll. 161–78)

Classic correctness has here harnessed the rambling simile into perfect propriety of language and of tight, flawless structure.

To discuss the content of Chapman's satiric verse is inevitably to consider his intellective ethic, for fundamentally it is directed toward one object: false learning. The scholar-poet took learning seriously—it was the heart of his whole philosophy of life—and

the many abuses of learning on the part of pedants, as well as
peasants, roused his ire more than any other subject. His scorn
for "learned ignorance" was quite as great as that for the detractors of genuine learning.

He mocks, as Sidney had before him, those "earth-creeping
minds" [12] that cannot appreciate poetry, but his language is more
aggressive and vitriolic:

> Forth then ye Mowles, sonnes of the earth abhorre her;
> Keepe still on in the durty vulgar way,
> Till durt receiue your soules, to which ye vow;
> And with your poison'd spirits bewitch your thrifts.
> Ye cannot so despise us as we despise you. ("To the Reader,"
> *Iliad*, ll. 139–44)

Even more than the merely ignorant or the simple scoffer at
knowledge, however, does the deliberate pedant, the self-styled
master of learning which is hollow and vain, come in for bitter
invective. For instance, there is his attack on the pedant's "learned
ignorance":

> So most learn'd Men, enough are Ignorant;
> But few the grace haue, to confesse their want,
> Till Liues, and Learnings, come concomitant.
> For from Mens knowledges; their Liues-Acts flowe;
> Vaineglorious Acts then, vaine proue all they know.
> As Night, the life-enclining starrs, best showes;
> So liues obscure, the starriest soules disclose.
> (Epilogue to the *Hymns*, ll. 69–75)

But Chapman's major manifesto of learning is "The Tears of
Peace" with an analysis of the nature and value of good learning
as well as an abomination of its abuses. Although the topical
framework of the poem is a protest against the war in the Netherlands, and although the "tears" allegorically represent the lamen-
tations of Peace over the death of Love, the central attack is on
the defective learning that brings about war through destroying
Love: "for good life is th'effect of Learnings act." In the *Inductio*
to this poem Chapman meets the spirit of Homer, his mentor;
and throughout Chapman maintains a personal tone that recalls
Samuel Daniel's defense of his art in *Musophilus*.[13]

According to Chapman, three kinds of men are foes to learning: the active, the passive, and the intellective. Active men scorn learning, expending their energies on soaring worldly ambitions:

> Your Actiue men, consume their whole lifes fire,
> In thirst of State-height, higher still and higher,
> (Like seeled Pigeons) mounting to make sport,
> To lower lookers on. (ll. 413–15)

At the opposite pole are the passive men who simply ignore learning while wasting their time in effete sensual indulgence: "In meates, and cuppes laborious; and take care / To lose without all care their Soule-spent Time" (ll. 430–31). But the most devastating foes are those supposedly "intellective" men of whom one would expect genuine love of learning, for they commit a worse offense than either scorning or ignoring it—they prostitute it:

> Your Intellectiue men, they study hard
> Not to get knowledge, but for meere rewarde.
> And therefore that true knowledge that should be
> Their studies end, and is in Nature free,
> Will not be made their Broker. (ll. 447–51)

Chapman then defines what he considers right learning, and the definition is Platonic and humanistic, in the tradition of Spenser and Milton:

> But this is Learning; To haue skill to throwe
> Reignes on your bodies powres, that nothing knowe;
> And fill the soules powers, so with act, and art,
> That she can curbe the bodies angrie part;
> All perturbations; all affects that stray
> From their one obiect; which is to obay
> Her Soueraigne Empire. (ll. 504–10)

The dynamic attitude toward learning as the way to a good life underlies virtually all of Chapman's satiric poetry, as well as his dramas. Rarely does his satire become personal, and only once does he permit private invective to intrude on his universal theme. Late in life he penned a diatribe against his old friend

Jonson, which was never published but was found in manuscript
form after the author's death. Supposedly responding to Jonson's
"Execration upon Vulcan," written after the fire which had de-
stroyed the contents of his desk, it sketches a vitriolic portrait
of conceited arrogance which, although in keeping with the
image of Jonson given us by others who quarreled with him, is
unrestrained in its acerbity. The poem, which begins with heavy
sarcasm, addresses the "most-greate-most-learn'd-wittie most /
Of all the kingdom"; makes several acrimonious references to
Jonson's notorious private aggressions ("didst thou not put out /
A boies Right eye that Croste thy mankind poute?"); and moves
on to a mocking paraphrase of the contents of the burned desk.
But even in this work Chapman seizes the opportunity for a
timely attack on false learning:

> Thes letterles Companions are not men
> With all the Arts and sciences Jndued,
> If of mans true and worthiest knowledge rude,
> Which is to knowe and be, one Compleat man,
> And that not all the swelling Ocean
> Of arts and sciences, cann poure both Jn. (ll. 188–93)

Like Matthew Arnold, Chapman scorned the Philistine who
parades his superficial learning for show. The external achievement of a degree is in itself futile, for genuine learning is within,
not without. In his stage comedies, as well as in his satiric poetry,
he mocked those fraudulent men of culture who "flutter in the
Blaze / Of ignorant count'nance; to obtaine degrees / And lye
in Learnings bottome, like the Lees, / To be accounted deepe, by
shallow men."

With its focus on the theme of learning and its consistent use
of the heroic couplet, Chapman's satiric verse is much more
unified than any of his other styles of poetry; uniformly effective,
it is his most consistently good style. Although Chapman was an
excellent satirist, however, he frequently imposed an allegorical
frame on his satire, to the detriment of the whole. In "The Tears
of Peace," for example, the allegorist usurps the introduction and
conclusion from the competent, controlled hand of the satirist.
The medieval roots of Chapman's consciousness at times undermine his superb satirical muse.

IV *The Allegorist*

As has been observed, Chapman was always a firm believer in "misteries and allegorical fiction." Most of his poetry is fundamentally allegorical in that it expresses one world in terms of another. Some of his verse, moreover, is formally and didactically allegorical in a manner which alienates him from the modern reader, who objects to allegory in its obvious medieval forms.[14] The medieval-minded poet who wrote "Eugenia," "The Shadow of Night," and "Andromeda Liberata" does not speak as directly to the contemporary mind as does either the metaphysical author of *Hero and Leander* or the satirical one of much of "The Tears of Peace."

Chapman's earliest publication is the allegorical poem *The Shadow of Night*. In the form of companion poems, "Hymn to Night" and "Hymn to Cynthia"—somewhat analogous to Milton's "Il Penseroso" and "L'Allegro"—it presents contrasting moods in a most unconventional manner. Contrary to the usual rhetorical denunciation of night, Chapman defends in the "Hymn to Night" the mystical darkness in opposition to the painted prostitute, fraudulent day. Lamenting the present degradation of daily life in this world, the poet longs for the ideal primordial chaos of darkness when all was "soule without a bodie." Now men are engulfed by "a stepdame Night of minde." In the "Hymn to Cynthia," addressed to the triple goddess—the moon, the world soul, and Queen Elizabeth—the overall allegory is elaborated around the allegorical myth of Acteon's hounds. Cynthia, depicted as a huntress, creates a nymph out of meteoric stuff whom she names Euthemia—representing contentment or inward joy—and who can herself assume "every shape of swiftest beasts." In the shape first of a panther, then of a boar, she draws men's base affections in hot pursuit. The Shadowy Hunting appears as a pageant of earthly desires. But the hounds do not bother Cynthia: they are merely her sport, and she disposes of them at night. True contentment is not the victory of those who pursue the daylight passions; it comes uninvited in the intellectual fulfillment of nightly solitude.

The poems are difficult and by reason of their topicality remain to some extent obscure. The allegorical interpretation of Acteon's hounds as the human passions was of course conventional in

Renaissance poetry, but in this essentially unconventional poem Chapman was concerned with attracting attention by composing a new variation on an old popular theme.[15] In a general way the allegory is clear enough, particularly in the light of thematic elements recurring throughout Chapman's work: his pervasive Platonic theme of the superiority of inward contentment, his aversion to the hurly-burly of the active life of the majority of men, and the religious implications of contemplative serenity. And the more specific allegorical interpretations suggested by some critics of the poem[16] run the danger of being more limiting than illuminating. Like Chapman's "painted light," they destroy the mysterious, undefinable glow so central to the vision of the poem.

Chapman also wrote two substantial elegies in allegorical form: *Eugenia* and *Epicedium*. *Eugenia*, in honor of Lord Russell, from whose influential family Chapman may have sought patronage, is not a consistently effective poem. The obvious allegorical structure is a dialogue of personified abstractions. Nobility seeks her sister Fame in the palace where she selects the room reserved for the illustrious Russell family. There she can retire in the company of the Graces and Virtues. In her subsequent encounter with Religion, she is prostrated by the sudden news of the Lord's death. But the best lines in the poem occur outside this allegorical frame: the account of Lord Russell's encounter with death is highly effective in its simple dignity, and the occasional digressions of doctrinal passages permit Chapman to expound admirably a favorite theory of correspondences. One is tempted to attribute the stiffness of much of the poem to the indifference of the poet to the personage under consideration, but the *Epicedium*, written for Prince Henry whom he genuinely loved and whose death was a personal misfortune for the poet, is equally unconvincing. Actually the poem is nearly a translation: most of it is a close paraphrase of a Latin elegy by Politian.[17] What Chapman added to his source reveals his heroic values: he inserted a lively account of Sir Thomas Gates' shipwreck in an expedition to Virginia, a contemporary tragedy which he compared to the calamity of the Prince's death. Both losses, though tragic, were mitigated by the heroism and nobility of the sufferers.

What should have been a happier event than the deaths which

evoked these two elegies was the wedding which occasioned Chapman's next allegorical poem, *Andromeda Liberata.* But the consequences both for the poet and the bridal pair were scarcely less funereal. Not only did the bride prove to be a murderess, but also this particular poem will always stand in Chapman's career as his unhappiest example of allegory. In spite of his unfortunate choice of the myth of Andromeda's liberation from the rock, he stubbornly defended his allegory in an angry prose retort to detractors of the poem who, he declared, simply could not read properly. And in the verse dialogue that follows the prose justification, Chapman has Theodines, the divinely inspired poet, exclaim in horrified incredulity over the misunderstood "barren rock": "as if that could applied be to a Man!" [18]

"The Tears of Peace" must also be included among Chapman's allegorical poems in spite of its substantial digressions into satire. The elaborate description of Love's funeral in the "Inductio" belongs to the medieval tradition of allegorical pageantry, because of the poem's personified abstractions (Love, Peace, Religion) and its symbolic beasts ("The woddes foure-footed Beasts, by two, and two; / A Male, and Female, matcht, of euerie kinde") in the cortege. And again near the end of the poem, after the satirical content of the middle, the allegorical frame reasserts itself as Peace confronts "the monster Murther." The allegorist has the last but not the best word.

On the whole Chapman's allegorical verse never achieved that harmonious balance between the "outer bark" and the "inner sap of Truth" which he asserted as its lofty intention. That triumph remained for Chapman the Classicist, who undertook the most divinely directed—and in a sense the most allegorically conceived—mission of all his poetic selves.

V *The Translator*

With eloquent simplicity, Chapman ends his translation of the works of Homer: "The work that I was born to do, is done." Ironically, this life-long task to which he felt divinely appointed by no less than the revered shade of Homer himself, has become the least familiar of Chapman's writings in the twentieth century. Although every schoolboy knows about the thrill that Keats felt "on looking into Chapman's Homer," only the rare scholar has himself dipped into this "realm of gold." And golden these books are.

Not as archaic and musty as their general oblivion might seem
to indicate, Chapman's versions of the two Homeric epics rank
very high in the long list of English translations since his time—
and his were the first. A century ago, Coleridge declared that
Chapman wrote as Homer might have written had he lived in
England in the reign of Queen Elizabeth. And in the twentieth
century Douglas Bush asserts that, "if Homer could return from
Elysium to read all the English renderings, he would surely find
in Chapman his truest son, a man who has fed on lion's mar-
row." [19] The vigor of language, perception of character, and
clarity of conception far outweigh the Chapmanesque Waterloos
of turgidity and obscurity. And, though his translations are
uneven and irregular, their dramatic power and sheer vitality
elevate them above Pope's elegant model of regularity and polish.
Chapman's Homer is briny and windswept; it is not a halcyon sea.

The *Iliad* and the *Odyssey* reveal striking technical differences
and some overall similarities in approach to theme and to the
art of translation. The *Iliad* was written in fourteeners, an old-
fashioned meter even for Chapman's day but one which he managed to handle with remarkable variety and flexibility. The
Odyssey was written in decasyllabic couplets, but skillful enjambement and artfully developed verse paragraphs save them
from monotony. Both epics were intended to translate the spirit
rather than the letter of Homer. As a result, Chapman permitted
himself to interpolate lines, to sharpen language, to refocus character, and to interpret action according to his own confirmed
vision of Homer's underlying intentions. His preface to the
Odyssey clarified his essentially allegorical view of the epics:
"The first word of his Iliads, is Μηνιν, *wrath:* the first word
of his Odysses, ανδρα, *Man:* contracting in either word, his
each workes Proposition. In one, *Predominant Perturbation;* in
the other, *ouer-ruling Wisedome:* in one, the Bodies feruour and
fashion of outward Fortitude, to all possible height of Heroicall
Action; in the other, the Minds inward, constant, and vncon-
querd Empire; vnbroken, vnalterd, with any most insolent, and
tyrannous infliction" (To the Earle of Somerset, ll. 1–9). In short,
the dualism of body and spirit that underlies most of Chapman's
verse finds its counterpart in the dual epics: the one concen-
trated on heroic physical action; the other, on the greater heroism
of inward fortitude.

The *Iliad* appeared in several strata, beginning with the publication of seven books in 1598 and ending with the completed
epic in 1611. An intervening revision which appeared in 1609
modified the initial version in the direction of greater clarity and
regularity, and the final product is on the whole much freer from
the seductive influence of verbal play—what Arnold called his
"fatal Cleopatra" [20]—than the first offering. The diction still
seems rather strange at first, but as one surrenders to the sweep
of the narrative, the strangeness dissipates into the color and vigor
demanded by the heroic subject. The racy Elizabethan flavor is
revealed in such descriptions as that of angry Juno: "and straight
her tongue had teeth in it, that wrought / This sharp invective"
(I, 521–22). The compound epithets out-Homer Homer in both
quantity and concreteness: "thump-buckler Mars," "dart-delight-
ing Queen," "great-high-deed-daring man." Colloquialisms spark
the narrative with informality—"good old Nestor" and "sound
stuff"—and humor is frequent: "Adrestus sought to save / His
head by losing of his feet and trusting to his knees" (IV, 42–43).

That Chapman introduces anachronisms into the text is not
at all surprising to anyone familiar with the clocks in Shakespeare's *Julius Caesar*. But the *Iliad* has not only its fairies and
its damask but its Elizabethan physiological theory complete
with abundant references to the "humours." Furthermore, in
keeping with Chapman's allegorical bent, personifications appear
often to give moral content to supernumerary deities and forces:
"contention" becomes "that black fiend" and demons become
devils. Because of these qualities Arnold objected that "between
Chapman and Homer there is interposed the mist of the fanciful-
ness of the Elizabethan age, entirely alien to the plain directness
of Homer's thought and feeling." [21] This objection is basically unfair, however, for the fancy is not misty but radiant and robust.

Confirmed allegorist and didactic writer that he was, Chapman
was more concerned with the moral significance of Homeric
heroes than with their esthetic coherence. As he proceeded with
his translation of the *Iliad*, the moral implications of the many
figures became more and more evident to him. At first he ad-
mired the wrathful Achilles and tried to rationalize his outbreaks
of passion; and the result is a somewhat modified, calmer, and
more learned hero than Homer portrays. Agamemnon is presented
in a much more blameworthy light than Achilles. But the in-

herently tragic figure of Hector appealed to Chapman more than
either of these two central roles, and he emerges, therefore, refined by moral heightening, as a stoic hero. All three are illuminated by the myth of Chapman's archetypal hero, Hercules. All
of his heroes—in the tragedies as well as in the epics—move
toward the blazing pyre where mortality will be purged and the
divine spirit freed to soar, unimpeded by flesh. Doomed, stoically
resigned Hector, is the central Herculean figure in the *Iliad*.
Among the minor figures, two interested Chapman as negative
exemplars: the effeminate Paris, whom he caricatures; and the
vapid Menelaus, whom he castigates. On the other hand, Glaucus,
whom Homer mocked, is defended by Chapman as a stoic figure.

The poet's extraordinarily deft handling of the bumpy fourteener is seen immediately in the following specimens:

> The Greeke host wondred at this Brave. Silence flew everywhere.
>   (III, 99)
> Quite through his skull: a hastie night shut up his latest day.
>   (IV, 489)
> Death with his purple finger shut, and violent fate, his eyes.
>   (V, 93)

Poetically Chapman's *Iliad* is a defiant triumph over an obstinate
meter. But it triumphs in other ways as well. A genuine epic, it
speaks with noble voice and moves with power and magnitude.
For example, Hector's farewell to Andromache:

> But neither Troy's posteritie so much my soule doth wound—
> Priam, nor Hecuba her selfe, nor all my brothers' woes
> (Who, though so many and so good, must all be food for foes)—
> As thy sad state, when some rude Greeke shall leade thee weeping
>   hence,
> These free dayes clouded and a night of captive violence
> Loding thy temples, out of which thine eyes must never see
> But spin the Greeke wives webs of taske and their Fetch-water be
> To Argos, from Messeides, or clear Hyperia's spring—
> Which (howsoever thou abhorst) Fate's such a shrewish thing
> She will be mistris, whose curst hands, when they shall crush out cries
> From thy oppressions (being beheld by other enemies)
> Thus they will nourish thy extremes: "This dame was Hector's wife,
> A man that, at the warres of Troy, did breathe the worthiest life

Of all their armie." This againe will rub thy fruitfull wounds
To misse the man that to thy bands could give such narrow bounds.
But that day shall not wound mine eyes: the solide heape of night
Shall interpose and stop mine eares against thy plaints and plight.

Chapman related that a new understanding came to him during
the course of translating the last twelve books of the *Iliad*, "in
which the first free light of my author entred and emboldened
me." The new light, which illuminated the heroism of Hector,
focused next on Odysseus as the fulfillment of the heroic ideal.
Regardless of personal preference, the reader of both epics cannot escape the sense that Chapman himself preferred the *Odyssey*.
The central theme of the *Odyssey*, the acquisition of learning
through experience, was inherently more sympathetic to the poet
than the Trojan war; and the long-suffering Odysseus even more
approaches Chapman's ideal of the truly learned man than did
Hector. As a result, Chapman's version of the physical adventures
of the *Odyssey* is allegorically an account of the spiritual adventures of regeneration and enlightenment.

Chapman's Odysseus is a dynamic figure. Far from being a
static moral ideal, he is portrayed throughout the epic as in the
process of acquiring wisdom and becomes the truly learned man
only through his rich experiences in the "sea of life." In the
evolutionary nature of his role, he reminds one very much of his
dynamic counterpart of the twentieth century, the hero of Nikos
Kazantzakis' *The Odyssey: A Continuation*. In a characteristically
Elizabethan way, Chapman's Odysseus is also dramatic in that
he is endowed with the *psychomachia*, or inner conflict, a medieval heritage which distinguished virtually all the tragic heroes
of Renaissance drama. Quite unlike Homer's hero, he is a self-
conscious figure, analytical and articulate on subjective matters.
Whereas the Homeric figure concentrates his keen mind on immediate physical problems, Chapman's hero carefully ponders
the subjective implications of each adventure. The poet focuses
all of his key speeches on the interpretation of the experience
involved, even contriving additional verses in elucidation of his
interpolated meaning. For example, in Book X, where the Homeric hero merely assesses a navigational problem, Chapman's
deduces the limitations of all human knowledge. Similarly, in
Odysseus' central speech to Athena when he lands in Ithaca—

also a key speech in the original—he adds eight lines of comment on the injustice of his sufferings and his resultant sense of spiritual isolation. And in his speech to Amphinous late in the epic—one of the rare examples of a subjective speech in Homer—Chapman's Odysseus asserts the value of suffering and the attainment of self-knowledge through insight into his challenging hardships. It is the tragic credo, and Chapman in effect transmutes the epic into tragedy by putting emphasis on the transcendent value of sufferings rather than on the final escape from them.

A recent and perceptive study of Chapman's *Odyssey* includes many useful observations about its complex allegory.[22] In Odysseus' spiritual struggle for self-mastery, the sea plays an important role; it is symbolic in its flux and violence of destructive natural forces and of the equally destructive and erratic human passions. Several episodes specifically represent the dangers which these passions threaten. The adventure on Circe's island reveals the danger of bestiality; the account of the sacking of Ismarus, that of the predatory instincts; the incident of the Lotus-eaters, that of gluttony; and blinding the Cyclops, that of irrationality. In relating each adventure, Chapman heightens the moral tone by shifting emphasis from the external arena of action to the inner stage of Odysseus' mind. At the same time he replaces the epic of triumph over adversity with a tragedy of wisdom through suffering. Odysseus' final victory over the sea and his return to Ithaca represent the victory of reason over passion, of permanence and stability (what Chapman calls "stay") over fluidity,[23] and of wisdom over success. The mood is one of tragedy, notwithstanding its untragic concluding episode.

As for Athena, the flashing-eyed goddess of Homer has become a more mystical figure, a subtle, rather elusive personification of Divine Wisdom. Her appearance before Odysseus is often vague and ghostly: she "stood over him, and had her presence given / A woman's form" (XX, 48–49). She approaches the sleeping Nausicaa "like a puft of wind" (IV, 28) and speeds to Telemachus' aid "swift as thought" (I, 170). But she remains, as in the original, "grey-eyed."

The style of the *Odyssey* is distinctive. At moments it surpasses anything in the *Iliad*, as when Odysseus returns home: "the sea had soaked his heart through." At others it outdoes the other

translation in turgidity: "and he / The acceptation author'd joy-
fully" (XV, 168–69). As in the case of the *Iliad*, Chapman
handles a rigid meter with remarkable flexibility. He avoids
monotony in the decasyllabic couplets through skillful use of
enjambement and the long verse paragraph. But he again goes
the *Iliad* one better in the use in the *Odyssey* of compound
epithets like "hony-sweetness-giving-minds-wine-fill'd." The diction is more varied than in the *Iliad*, including Latinate words
alongside colloquialisms; and throughout there is a much heavier
concentration of metaphorical language. In diction and tone the
Odyssey is much closer to the metaphysical Chapman than is the
Iliad. Not only the extensive use of metaphor, sometimes as
conceit, but the abundance of rhetorical devices and the frequent
elliptical expressions make for an intellectual poetry quite different from that of the more resonant *Iliad*.

After the major achievement of the *Odyssey*, Chapman turned
to the task of translating the minor Homeric poems. But intent
merely on "finishing off" [24] his Homer, he did not approach the
level of the epics in his rendering of the *Batrachomyomachia*,
the *Hymns*, and the *Epigrams*. Their poetic shortcomings are
both positive and negative: not only do they lack the fire and
the vigor which sustain the epics, but they also surrender completely to the strained and circumlocutionary language which
elsewhere only slightly mars Chapman's verse. Their best moments come through the neo-Classic satirical vein of the poet, as
when Chapman, identifying himself with poor, underesteemed
Homer, looses fire at the vulgar herd of his detractors:

> And what's all their skill but vast varied reading?
> As if brode-beaten High-waies had the leading
> To Truth's abstract, and narrow Path and Pit,
> Found in no walk of any worldly wit.
> And without Truth, all's onely slight of hand,
> Or our Law-Learning in a Forraine Land,
> Embroderie spent on Cobwebs, Braggart show
> Of men that all things learn and nothing know.

If not exactly Homeric, these words are appropriately heroic.

In addition to the Homeric works, Chapman published at least
three other translations from the Greek: the *Works and Days*

of Hesiod, the *Hero and Leander* of Musaeus, and the fifth satire
of Juvenal. The georgic of Hesiod, a substantial undertaking of
some thirteen hundred lines, was dedicated to Sir Francis Bacon
in 1618. As the title page ponderously explains, it contains "Doctrine of Husbandrie, Moralitie, and Pietie; with a perpetuall
Calendar of Good and Bad Daies; Not superstitious, but neces-
sarie (as farre as naturall Causes compell) to observe." These
moralizing heroic couplets are far from representing Chapman's
best vein of poetry, and the footnotes—querulous, pedantic, or
quaint—often prove more absorbing than the text. Perhaps Chapman felt drawn to Hesiod because the Greek poet felt cheated
of his proper inheritance by his brother, whom he reproves in
the early stanzas. The *Divine Poem* of Musaeus, dedicated to
Inigo Jones in 1616, treats the subject of Hero and Leander
again; but this time Chapman translated the Greek version rather
than interpreted the legend originally. A few lines are borrowed
from the earlier sestiads, however, and they are by far the best
lines in the poem. Finally, Chapman published in 1629 "A just
reproofe of a Romane Smell-Feast, being the fifth satyre of
Juvenal," appended to a brief prose tour-de-force, "A Justification of a Strange Action of Nero, in burying one of the cast
Hayres of his Mistresse Poppaea." Always congenial to satire,
Chapman succeeds in both works; but, whereas the uneven poem
does not equal his earlier verse, the essay makes one wish he had
written much more prose. Although the content of the Nero piece
is slight,[25] it involves a dramatic episode; and Chapman was
basically a dramatic writer.

Substantial content and technical versatility render the poetry
of George Chapman both significant and interesting, but its
greatness is sporadic rather than sustained. Certainly the Homeric translations are, as William Godwin remarked long ago,
one of the greatest treasures the English language has to boast.
Although a copybook of exquisite lines could easily be culled
from his original verse, his poetry gives the impression at times
of being labored. But, if Chapman the poet struggled to dig his
poems from "this fowl Panther earth," Chapman the playwright
flew with ease on the wings of an unerring theatrical instinct.

CHAPTER 3

Of Humorous Mirth

A READING of Chapman's comedies readily refutes the long standing fallacy that he was essentially a non-dramatic poet who wrote only reluctantly for the theater. Contrary to the usual handbook assertions,[1] his plays—particularly the comedies—seem written by natural instinct rather than by will. The seven extant specimens of his comic drama rank easily with the productions of Middleton, Marston, and Jonson; and they all exemplify the remarkable Elizabethan gift for theatricality at its liveliest. Chapman's particular flair was, in fact, specifically theatrical rather than dramatic. Total structure was his weak point, but his plays abound in great scenes; and time after time he transmuted a static episode into a superb *coup de théâtre*.

Chapman began his dramatic career as a writer of comedies. This initial comic phase, which occupied only the decade of 1595–1605, was characterized by a keen responsiveness to the shifting dramatic trends of the time. His earliest plays experimented with the comedy of "humours"—a popular fashion that he introduced and helped to develop—but his later pieces turned in the disparate directions of satire and romance where he again made significant original contributions. Although Jonson's *Every Man in His Humour* is often erroneously credited with initiating "humorous" comedy, Chapman's *Blind Beggar* launched the new mode on the London stage in 1595. Derived from the contemporary physiological theory of the four "humours" as dominant influences on human personality, such comedy exploited the "humour" as a ruling and distorting passion that severely unbalanced a personality in one particular direction. In the words of Jonson: "Some one peculiar quality / Doth so possess a man, that it doth draw / All his affects, his spirits, and his powers, / In their confluctions, all to run one way."[2] As exaggerated emotions, such as jealousy, the "humours" were readily adapted to satire;

but frequently they took the form of a mere mannerism, indicative of the follies but not of the vices of men. The *Blind Beggar* was followed by *A Humorous Day's Mirth* (1597), *All Fools* (1599), and *May Day* (*ca.* 1601), all essentially "humour" plays; then by *Sir Giles Goosecap* (*ca.* 1602), a transitional play with the "humours" relegated to a subplot and with a main plot devoted to the romance, a new comic mode.

I   Blind Beggar of Alexandria

The Blind Beggar of Alexandria, the first extant play definitely attributed to Chapman, was performed by the Lord Admiral's Men at Henslowe's theater, the Rose, in the 1595–96 season. It was highly successful; twenty-two performances are recorded in Henslowe's Diary, and there were more after its revival in 1601. Only a few all-time favorites, such as Marlowe's *Doctor Faustus* and Thomas Kyd's *Spanish Tragedy,* exceed this record. In spite of its popularity, or perhaps because of the lopsided popularity of its farcical subplot, it appeared in print in 1598 in badly mutilated form with only about sixteen hundred lines remaining of what was obviously a much longer stage play. The title page of this version, as published by William Jones, reveals an emphasis on the comic half of the action which may account for the virtual disappearance of the romantic half: *The Blinde Beggar of Alexandria, most pleasantly discoursing his variable humours in disguised shapes full of concite and pleasure.*

Although no specific source is known for the truncated romantic story of *The Blind Beggar,* the materials are obviously those of the late Greek romance: magic, sorcery, mythical transformations. The principal figures in this plot are the old King Ptolemy; his young wife Aegiale, who yields to an adulterous passion for the warrior Cleanthes; Ptolemy's daughter Aspasia, who is advised by an oracle to wed Prince Doricles of Arcadia; and four neighboring kings who invade Egypt. Prince Doricles is murdered by Cleanthes; Aegiale and Aspasia are no less finally disposed of by textual corruption; and the fragmentary plot remains unresolved. Nor has a definite source been found for the fairly complete subplot involving the many disguises and adventures of Irus, the blind beggar named after his counterpart in the *Odyssey;* but the disguise theme involves episodes of comic trickery which are stock items of the contemporary stage.

In one sense the *Blind Beggar* was an old-fashioned play for its time. It contains several instances of the hallowed morality device of direct address to the audience, which serves the double purpose of entertainment and exposition. As exposition, this device, which had suited the homiletic apron stage of the medieval morality, remained as a vestigial technique in much early Elizabethan drama; and Chapman never wholly abandoned it in his comedies. Several examples of the introductory monologue of self-exposition occur, as when Irus, in the opening scene, explains his multiple role to the audience: "I am Cleanthes and blind Irus too, / And more than these, as you shall soon perceive" (i, 110–11). He then announces that he is also Leon the usurer, and the madcap nobleman Count Hermes. He concludes by clarifying his intentions to the audience:

> For, till the time that I may claim the crown,
> I mean to spend my time in sports of love,
> Which in the sequel you shall plainly see,
> And joy, I hope, in this my policy. (i, 123–26)

An example of the merely entertaining aside occurs when Irus, disguised as Count Hermes and speaking of someone ill with the "knave's evil," turns abruptly to the audience to ask, with a touch of homiletic irony, "Which of you are troubled with that disease, masters?"

In another sense, however, the *Blind Beggar* represented an innovation on the Elizabethan stage. As noted above, it introduced the popular convention of "humour" comedy in English drama. Irus belabors the word in an early soliloquy as he dons "the humour of a wild and frantic man," Count Hermes, "whose humours five summers I have held." With the exception of Irus, however, who is convincing in the chameleon "humours" of his multiple role, the characterization suffers from the arbitrary imposition of the "humour" device on otherwise static figures.

The principals of the main plot are mere puppets, with the single exception of Queen Aegiale, her Phaedra-like role heightened by the consuming passions of her illicit love. Most of the minor characters are conventional types: Pego, the buffoon; Bragadino, the braggart; Elimine, the snobbish social climber. But the versatile hero, in his fourfold manifestations as beggar,

nobleman, usurer, and soldier, is an effective prototype of the
intriguer who assumes the central role in all of Chapman's subsequent comedies. Unlike his ultimate ancestor, the clever and
energetic Vice of the morality drama, he is not evil but amoral.
His intrigues are entirely gratuitous, a matter of "sport." He may
even be guilty of committing crimes—indeed, he kills Prince
Doricles—but murder is quickly forgotten in the amoral comic
world of this intriguer. In the absence of moral context, judgment
does not exist and deeds bear no consequences. This manipulating protagonist also resembles the Vice in his inherent theatricality: he is above all a great actor. He is not only a quick-change
artist in disguise but skilled enough in leading his quadruple life
to deceive simultaneously two wives and a mistress.

The language of the play, a combination of prose and blank
verse, is by no means distinguished. On occasion, however, Chapman endows even a time-worn convention of Elizabethan imagery with original lyric beauty:

> Out of my treasury choose th[y] choice of gold,
> Till thou find some matching thy hair in brightness;
> But that will never be, so choose thou ever.
> Out of my jewelry choose thy choice of diamonds,
> Till thou find some as brightsome as thine eyes;
> But that will never be, so choose thou ever.
> Choose rubies out until thou match thy lips,
> Pearl till thy teeth, and ivory till thy skin
> Be match'd in whiteness, but that will never be;
> Nor never shall my treasury have end,
> Till on their beauties ladies loathe to spend;
> But that will never be, so choose thou ever. (v, 104–15)

And at times a flash of comic vigor gives an intimation of the
later Chapman's skilled dialogue, as when Bragadino asks of
the Count, who has demanded his identity: "what art thou that
hast the guts of thy brains grip'd with such famine of knowledge
not to know me?" (ii, 25–27). For the most part, however, the
style is flat.

Standing out sharply in this predominantly plain style are frequent paraphrases and echoes of Marlovian language, and a close
examination of the play reveals episodic as well as verbal echoes
of Chapman's younger contemporary. Several verbal parallels

derive from Marlowe's poetry rather than his plays. Hermes offers
a pastoral proposal to Aspasia in the manner of Marlowe's passionate shepherd:

> But come, sweet love, if thou wilt come with me,
> We two will live amongst the shadowy groves,
> And we will sit like shepherds on a hill,
> And with our heavenly voices tice the trees
> To echo sweetly to our celestial tunes.
> Else will I angle in the running brooks,
> Seasoning our toils with kisses on the banks;
> Sometime I'll dive into the murmuring springs,
> And fetch thee stones to hang about thy neck,
> Which by thy splendour will be turn'd to pearl. (ix, 24–33)

And King Brebitious echoes *Hero and Leander* in the final scene
when he spontaneously approves of the wife bestowed on him
by Cleanthes: "None ever lov'd, but at first sight they lov'd"
(x, 130).

Along with the verbal parallels, the shadows of several Marlovian heroes also fall in close fitting fashion over the various
roles of the blind beggar. Irus identifies himself as "a shepherd's
son at Memphis born," an ancestry resembling that of Tamburlaine; and, like him, he becomes king despite his lowly origins.
In his disguise as Leon the usurer, who "cast his desperate body
/ From the Alexandrian Tower into the sea" (x, 53–54), Irus
pursues the career and achieves the death of Barrabas, the Jew of
Malta, who plunged to his fate in a cauldron. As Count Hermes,
whose name evokes the whole mystical and magical tradition
surrounding Hermes Trismegisthus, Irus shares the castastrophic
death of Marlowe's magician, Faustus; falling to damnation, he
is swallowed in the gaping earth:

> Where hell to interrupt his passage thither,
> Raving beneath the groundwork of the earth,
> As if ten thousand vapours burst in her,
> Severed her womb and swallowed quick
> The miserable Count. (ix, 106–110)

Although deliberate parody of Marlowe cannot be proven, these
concrete analogies offer strong evidence that such was Chapman's

intention in his first play.[3] And, although such a fragmentary piece cannot be judged as a whole, the remnants of *The Blind Beggar of Alexandria* serve not only to point some of the main directions in Chapman's comic dramaturgy but also to predict his future mastery of a genuine comic gift.

II A Humorous Day's Mirth

A Humorous Day's Mirth opened at the Rose Theatre in 1597, and thirteen performances are recorded by Henslowe. There may well have been more, but a gap in the diary at about this time deprives scholars of evidence. The play was published in quarto in 1599 as *A pleasant Comedy entituled: An Humerous Dayes Myrth*.

Although this second comedy of Chapman's exists in a very corrupt text, it has major historical importance as the first complete comedy of "humours," fulfilling that conception of comedy only touched upon in *The Blind Beggar*. Its intrinsic value as a play is slight, however, for the exposition and mockery of "humours" is for the most part mechanical and repetitious. With his usual weakness for overcrowding the stage with supernumeraries, Chapman introduces several gallants displaying the same "humour," that of aping the speeches of gentlemen. At times, however, he heightens his pageant of mimicry with the trusty device of dramaturgic contrast. The "humour" of jealousy is so formulated. The elderly gentleman Labervele, fawning and solicitous yet highly suspicious of his beautiful young Puritan wife, is balanced against the vituperous and violently jealous old woman Countess Moren, who browbeats her youthful husband. Still another dramatic foil is offered in the person of Foyes, who jealously guards his attractive daughter Martia from all suitors except Labesha, the wealthy dolt whom he wishes her to marry.

A thematic dimension joins the "humour" comedy and dramaturgic contrast in the juxtaposition of Dowsecer the scholar and Labesha the pedant. In this way Chapman objectifies his favorite theme, the opposition of genuine and false learning. Dowsecer's "humour" is melancholy, but his is the philosophical melancholy of the scholar, not the moodiness of the eccentric. His melancholy involves an introspective and idealistic condemnation of this world and its vanities, wherein he bears a striking resemblance to his famous fellow student, Hamlet.[4] Dowsecer's central soliloquy on the subject, occurring in the seventh scene, bears close analysis. The friends who invade his solitude with the intention of mocking his melancholy are converted to respect (and the heroine Martia to love) when they hear his profound reaction to the worldly objects of temptation placed in his way—a sword, a codpiece, and a portrait of a lady.

The melancholy he expresses is not merely temperamental but reveals a philosophical attitude toward the world. He begins by citing Chapman's old favorite, Cicero, translating as follows: "What can seem strange to him on earthly things / To whom the whole course of eternity, / And the round compass of the world is known?" (vii, 67–69). Seizing the sword placed before him, Dowsecer scoffingly catalogues base means of dying, the shameless world's "gross ensigns of her levity": "As if there were not ways enough to die / By natural and casual accidents, / Diseases, surfeits, brave carouses, old aqua-vitae, and too base wives, / And thousands more" (vii, 96–99). Piqued by the sight of the hose and codpiece, he then continues in a satirical vein, enumerating the follies of men and the absurdities of their fashions. The lady's picture, on the other hand, inspires him to a witty and paradoxical defense of the use of cosmetics.

When he then suddenly discovers his father's concealed presence in the room, he abruptly denounces marriage, citing himself as an example of the futility of parenthood. But almost as quickly the sight of Martia transforms the brooding scholar into a longing lover: "thou has not changed / My soul to sense, but sense unto my soul" (vii, 213–14). For her part Martia is already willing to die with him, and the king admiringly explains to the audience: "This is no humour, this is but perfit judgment" (vii, 88). Dowsecer has the genuine Platonic gift of divine madness—"as of a holy fury, not a frenzy" (vii, 198).

In contrast to the genuine scholar, the pedant Labesha exemplifies the superficial, empty knowledge that Chapman railed against in his poetry. He pretentiously parades foreign phrases out of context, then misinterprets Martia's Latin declination of *Moto, motas*—"O excellent! She hath called him ass in Latin" (v, 82). He misuses polysyllabic words but subsides into inarticulate whimpering when challenged by the clever Lemot. As a result of his foolish pose, he is despised and mocked by everyone in the play.

The silly Labesha, whose "soul is in sense," is incapable of scoffing at sensual temptation as did Dowsecer; but he gets his chance in a temptation scene which ingeniously parallels the one staged for the real scholar. The cue to Labesha's temptation is given by Dowsecer when he refers to those men, "when like to cream-bowls, all their virtues swim / In their set faces" (vii, 131–32). When Labesha adopts the melancholy "humour" in order to parade his futile love for Martia, his friend Catalien sets before him "a mess of cream, a spice-cake, and a spoon, as the armor, picture, and apparel was set in the way of Dowsecer" (xii, 24–26). His initial response seems scholarly enough: he quotes in Latin an old proverb he remembered "ever since he read his accidence" (xii, 33–34). But his subsequent translation is facetious: "Oh, silly state of things, for things they be that cause this silly state. And what is a thing?" (xiii, 35–37). His speculation on the nature of things is cut short by the sudden sight of the cream. Mixing spoonfuls of cream with protestations of regret, he downs the delicacy, declaring "To end my life eat I this cream and cake" (xii, 52). Discovered in the midst of his indulgence, he falters in embarrassment. After this key scene, Labesha virtually disappears from the play; his function is fulfilled.

Florilla, the main female role, is an early example of stage satire aimed at the Puritan sect. She is a convincing and well-developed character in spite of the basic element of caricature in her portrayal. A stuffy but apparently sincere young woman who observes extreme austerity in clothing, she sternly refuses even the jewels and the velvet gown urged upon her by her aging husband. But under the Puritanical surface of her demeanor lurks a gay sprite waiting to be freed. And when Lemot, the manipulator-hero of the play, urges her to test her cloistered virtue by exposing it to the temptations of the court, she quickly consents, betraying the sensuality hidden beneath the pious pose. With unexpected wit she cites scriptural justification of her loose behavior from the fourth chapter of Habbakuk—a book with only three chapters!

Her abrupt change in character is not achieved entirely without

conflict, however; the intellectual young lady engages in a dialogue between herself and reason, assuming the viewpoint of her
husband Labervele!

> Reason, shall I endure a desolate man to come
> And court my wife, and prove her constancy?
> *Reason:* "To court and prove her you may bear, my lord,
> For perfit things are not the worse for trial;
> Gold will not turn to dross for deepest trial."
> Before God a comfortable saying.
> Thanks, gentle Reason, I'll trouble you no more. (vi, 27–33)

Having so rationalized, she joins the daring party at the tavern
arranged by Lemot. But, when the tricky Lemot threatens to
expose her escapade, she slips home to don again her Puritan
grey, complete with matching mask of righteous indignation, to
greet her husband's all too accurate suspicions. Nothing has
changed for Florilla: the Puritan hypocrisy remains.

A *Humorous Day's Mirth* obtains its unity and coherence not
so much from the satirical theme as from its intriguer-hero Lemot,
who supervises the paradox of "humours" and manipulates the
disparate characters in a highly complex plot. Lemot initiates a
series of intrigues which lead to a complete entanglement of the
disparate threads of plot. After persuading Florilla to test her
virtue, he invites her to meet him at a tavern, and to bring with
her Martia to meet the King (who remains unnamed in the play).
He then persuades Countess Moren to permit her husband to
dine at the same tavern, but on the condition that no women
will be present. At the tavern, when Moren joins the King and
the two ladies in a private room, Lemot dashes off to tell both
the Countess and Count Labervele of the shocking behavior of
their respective marital partners. When they rush to the tavern,
they arrive at the same time as Foyes and Labesha, and the
party is broken up in utter confusion, with Florilla escaping
undetected and Martia carried off by the King. To complete his
trickery, Lemot then undertakes to inform the Queen of the
King's escapade, amplifying it with an account of an attack on
the royal kidnapper by the outraged lover, Dowsecer; and the
Queen hastens to the tavern to rescue her husband. As all these
characters converge on the tavern, Lemot clarifies the multiple

errors and restores order; and the play ends festively with a
pageant and lottery.

Like his predecessor Irus, Lemot announces his intention both
explicitly and immediately: "I will sit like an old king in an old-
fashion play, . . . and point out all my humourous companions"
(ii, 12–13, 20–21). Unlike Irus, however, Lemot has not even the
nominal personal motives of ambition or of lust: he engages in
trickery for the "sport" and "the jest of it," and his enjoyment of
it is purely intellectual. Not even a hint of sensuality invades his
clever seduction into society of Florilla, the cloistered Puritan.

Lemot too is a scholar. Even in argument with the erudite
Florilla he proves to be "an obscure and philosophical scholar."
A wit as well, he engages, in keeping with the spirit of his name,
in continual verbal play. He endows the otherwise undistin-
guished prose of the dialogue with the vitality of his puns and
word-combats. Above all he is a superb actor, capable of ad-
libbing his way out of every serious crisis with almost Falstaffian
ingenuity. Along with a touch of the Restoration gallant about
him lingers a strong flavor of the morality Vice. Not only is he
called "monsieur Sathan," "vicar of hell," and several such demonic epithets, but his amusement is at times Gothic and grim,
in the traditional medieval manner. He boasts, for instance, that:
"my father and my mother died both in a day, and I rung me
a peal for them, and they were no sooner brought to the church
and laid in their graves, but I fetched me two or three fine capers
aloft, and took my leave of them, as men do of their mistresses
at the ending of a gaillard" (xi, 51–55). Yet he remains also an
aristocrat and courtier, the "minion of the king."

Lemot anticipates a succession of imaginative, energetic, and
learned young men who in Chapman's later plays deftly manipulate the multiple plot threads in their respective dramatic vehicles.
A Humorous Day's Mirth is thus a paradigm of Chapman's comedy both in its plot and its protagonist.

III All Fools

All Fools, an excellent comedy far surpassing its predecessors
in Chapman's canon, opened on the boards of the Rose Theatre
in 1599 but moved to the Blackfriars shortly thereafter when
Chapman transferred his services to the Children of the Chapel.
A successful play before both a sophisticated and a popular audi-

ence, it was also given court performance "before his Majesty" on New Year's Night, 1604–5.

Unlike the earlier comedies, this play has detectable sources. Chapman, who turned to the Latin drama for the plot of *All Fools*, cleverly combined elements of three separate plays of Terence. The main line of action is borrowed directly from the *Heautontimorousmenos*, a conventional Terentian comedy involving a pair of fathers, one strict and one indulgent; a pair of sons; and an enterprising slave who masterminds the amorous intrigues of the sons in order to deceive the fathers. Supplementing the main plot are relevant episodes, as will be noted, from two other Terentian plays, *Adelphi* and *The Eunuch*. But this use of sources did not inhibit Chapman's originality. Not content merely to borrow a Classic play and adapt it superficially to the English stage, the Elizabethan dramatist completely changed and enormously vitalized the original play, as a result of which it is one of the most successful instances of Latin comedy transformed into Elizabethan theater. Much can be learned about Chapman's dramaturgy from an analysis of the changes he wrought on his sources, as these changes, both basic and pervasive, affect plot structure, language, and characterization.

Chapman modified the Terentian plot in two important ways. For one, he added a subplot. In handling the main action he abandoned a pageant of "humours" in favor of an organic, complex structure of intrigue; but, rather than discard humour comedy altogether, he incorporated into a subplot the absurdly "humorous" jealousy of Cornelio, a would-be cuckold who quite unjustifiably suspects his wife Gazetta of amorous adventures. Associated with this couple in the subplot are three other figures: the amorous courtier Dariotto, who has ambitions to justify Cornelio's suspicions; and a pair of pedants, a notary and a doctor. Dariotto is vividly drawn: a diligent philanderer, he pursues his foppish mode of life with zesty wit and supercilious poise. He is a precursor of such a Restoration gallant as Sir Fopling Flutter. The notary and the doctor continue Chapman's comic campaign against false learning: these pedants serve as foils to Rinaldo, the young scholar-intriguer who replaces the wily slave in Terence; and they appear in one scene each, for the sole purpose of performing their single stints of satire. The doctor, Pock, who is appropriately named, is glib in offering fancy diagnoses—

"The incision is not deep, nor the orifice exorbitant; the peri-
cranion is not dislocated" (III, i, 392–93)—but he admits to the
same sort of chicanery found in the legal profession: "cures are
like causes in law, which may be lengthened or shortened at the
discretion of the lawyer" (III, i, 407–8). The notary, as if in
confirmation of such practices, reads a verbose bill of divorce-
ment:

notwithstanding all former contracts, covenants, bargains, conditions,
agreements, compacts, promises, vows, affiances, assurances, bonds,
bills, indentures, poll-deeds, deeds of gift, defeasances, feoffments,
endowments, vouchers, double vouchers, privy entries, actions, declara-
tions, explications, rejoinders, surrejoinders, rights, interests, demands,
claims, or titles whatsoever, heretofore betwixt the one and the other
party, or parties, being had, made, passed, convenanted, and agreed,
from the beginning of the world till the day of the date hereof.
(IV, i, 321–30)

Also included in the subplot for the benefit of the Blackfriars
audience is literary parody that catered to its urbane taste. In
the middle of the play a page intrudes upon the action to deliver
a witty discourse to Cornelio on the innate imperfections of
women, in language obviously modeled on Lyly's euphuistic style
for it is rich in antitheses and analogies: "allow the prickle for
the rose, the brack for the velvet, / the paring for the cheese, and
so forth." [5] The page's role, an obvious interpolation, was probably
inserted after the move to the private theater.

The other, more important modification of the original plot
structure is Chapman's incorporation of a moral dimension. The
Latin play is basically amoral: the only recognized good and evil
are success and failure. The hero of the *Eunuch*, for instance,
blithely boasts his rape of a virgin to whose room he had gained
access by disguising himself as a eunuch. Neither regret on his
part nor reproach from any one else is forthcoming. But the
Renaissance dramatists, writing as they did in the Christian tradition, imposed a moral scheme on their Classic, pagan sources:
time and again, for example, an "inherited" prostitute was transformed to a wife on the English stage. Chapman likewise in this
play converted the courtesan Bacchis into the secret wife Gratiana,[6] and he even established the entire amorous intrigue of
the play within the context of marriage and gave the gallants

honorable intentions. Furthermore, the parental relationships are cast in a moral mold: each father is genuinely concerned with the propriety of his son's ethical training and behavior. Marc Antonio has misgivings about the effect of his leniency on his rebellious son, and Gostanzo, although deceived in thinking so, is sincerely proud of the scion whom he believes to be so serious, thrifty, and modest. Even the intriguer Rinaldo is not merely modernized to replace the stock figure of the wily slave, but also moralized so that he manipulates his trickery with philosophical, even scholarly, reflection, and never descends to any really dishonorable action.

The heightened characterization in Chapman's adaptation of Terence results in part from this same moral dimension. Furthermore, unlike the stereotyped characters and stock situations in the Terentian play, Chapman's highly individualized figures engage in actions which evolve organically from the given comic situation. Plot grows out of character, and a series of episodes results naturally from the ruling passions that dominate each of his main figures. The two fathers, for example, are constrasted not merely from the viewpoint of their educational theories but also in their temperaments. Marc Antonio, the indulgent parent, is modest and retiring in manner, and also the very epitome of naïveté: extremely gullible, he is the first to be made fool of in this play where all are fools. Gostanzo, the strict father, is just the opposite; for both miserly and hypocritical, he manifests an overweening self-conceit, as illustrated when he boasts to his son of his courtly skills as a young man; and he also prides himself on a certain shrewdness in dealings with his fellow men.

The two sons, much alike, achieve very different reputations. Fortunio, in spite of the rift with his father over his defiant marriage, is actually a much more obedient son than Valerio, who has deluded his strict father into thinking him the complete opposite of the worldly gallant that he in reality is. Valerio is the best-developed character in the play, stealing the scene even from the masterminding Rinaldo. A lively, colorful example of the Renaissance gallant, Valerio is skilled in music, sonneteering, eloquence —and drinking and dicing. But most of all he loves to show off: "My spirit longs to swagger" (II, i, 226). As a result, he lets himself be gulled into an exhibition of his dancing: "If you will have it, I must needs confess / I am no husband of my qualities" (II, i,

396–97). But, unlike the Restoration gallant whom he also anticipates,[7] Valerio is relatively innocent: a Mercutio in his high
spirits and verbal zest, he is a Romeo in his romantic idealism.
He professes a Platonic devotion to Love:[8]

> I tell thee Love is Nature's second sun
> Causing a spring of virtues where he shines;
> And as without the sun, the world's great eye,
> All colours, beauties, both of Art and Nature,
> Are given in vain to men; so without Love
> All beauties bred in women are in vain,
> All virtues born in men lie buried;
> For Love informs them as the sun doth colours. (I, i, 97–104)

But Valerio also states the cynical theme of the play: "For I see
all the world is but a gull, / One man gull to another in all kinds"
(II, i, 360–361). And he speaks the last word in the final scene
when he leaps onto a chair and, with his characteristic love of
theatricality, delivers a mock discourse of ninety-eight lines on
"the horned age."

The central figure (in the role performed by the intriguing
slave in the Latin drama) is Rinaldo, the younger brother of
Fortunio and the rival in wit to Valerio. Rinaldo is of the lineage
of Lemot and, like all of Chapman's comic heroes, prides himself
on being a scholar. In the opening scene, he echoes the traditional scholarly cynicism about women. Didactically he incorporates it in a philosophical view concerning the illusoriness of
beauty:

> And what is Beauty? A mere quintessence,
> Whose life is not in being, but in seeming;
> And therefore is not to all eyes the same,
> But like a cozening picture, which one way
> Shows like a crow, another like a swan.
> And upon what ground is this beauty drawn?
> Upon a woman, a most brittle creature,
> And would to God (for my part) that were all. (I, i, 44–51)

Gostanza recognizes in this young scholar a more admirable son
than his brother Fortunio who wantonly yielded to marriage:
"You have a younger son at Padua, / I like his learning well,

make him your heir, / And let your other walk" (I, i, 315–17).
Perhaps Chapman—who added the younger brother to the original cast of characters—identified himself wistfully with this
scholarly "second son," just as he had with the melancholy and
learned Dowsecer.

Although Rinaldo scoffs at those in the throes of love, he readily advances his erudition in the service of the tormented lovers
for the sheer sport of intrigue. He devises an ingenious plan of
deception whereby both young couples can live together secretly
under the very eyes of Gostanza: "Down on your knees, poor
lovers, reverence learning! / . . . Mark what cause / Flows from
my depth of knowledge to your loves, / To make you kneel and
bless me while you live" (I, ii, 86, 88–89). Like his predecessors
Irus and Lemot, Rinaldo defines his role in the play in the conventional soliloquy of self-revelation; like his successors Tharsalio
(*The Widow's Tears*) and the tragic Bussy, he both invokes and
challenges the goddess Fortuna:

> Fortune, the great commandress of the world,
> Hath divers ways to advance her followers:
> To some she gives honour without deserving,
> To other some, deserving without honour;
> Some wit, some wealth, and some wit without wealth;
> Some wealth without wit, some nor wit nor wealth,
> But good smock-faces, or some qualities
> By nature without judgment, with the which
> They live in sensual acceptation,
> And make show only, without touch of substance.
> My fortune is to win renown by gulling. (V, i, 1–11)

But in this play of fools, even the clever Rinaldo is gulled. Ironically, his daring wit is foiled by no less than the vengeful Cornelio, who mocks the young man's boasted scholarship:

> Go, shallow scholar, you that make all gulls,
> . . . This gull to him
> And to his fellow guller shall become
> More bitter than their baiting of my humour;
> . . . (although I be no scholar)
> Yet have I thus much Latin, as to say
> *Jam sumus ergo pares.* (V, i, 58, 61–63, 73–75)

The master guller admits that he has at last overreached himself, "What a dull slave was I to be thus gull'd!" (V, ii, 80); but he is already looking forward to counter-intrigue: "Perhaps my friend, or I, before we part, / May make even with you" (V, ii, 84–85).

As well as enriching the characterization and moralizing the plot structure of his sources, Chapman rhetorically heightened the polished but plain language of the Terentian originals. Terence depended largely upon the complex plot for comic effect, but Chapman's adaptation gains considerably from the vigorous Elizabethan idiom of its poetry. The play is written in easy, fluent blank verse; and this language often combines with brilliantly contrived situations to achieve superb moments of high comedy as in the "confession" scene. Rinaldo's ingenuity stages a mock confession by Valerio (which happens to be true) which receives in turn a mock forgiveness from his father (which is not intended to be true). The jest so delicately balances illusion and reality that Gratiana fears for a moment that her husband is actually jeopardizing their marriage; and Gonzago, who has feigned forgiveness only for the benefit of the bewildered Marc Antonio, is utterly nonplussed when he learns that the confession was not part of the act as he had thought and that he cannot gracefully recant the words that he acted so well when no one else present was acting at all!

Swinburne was not alone in considering *All Fools* Chapman's best comedy.[9] Such scenes as the one above illustrate the playwright's keen sense of theatricality, and the play as a whole skillfully interweaves character and comic situation in a manner that recalls those familiar comic masterpieces of his rival Jonson, *Epicene* and *The Alchemist*. What Swinburne called "a fresh and radiant air of mirth and light swift buoyancy of life" not only distinguish *All Fools* from the usual brittle versions of Latin New Comedy at that time but charm even a twentieth-century audience. With this play Chapman had moved from mere "humour" to high comedy.

IV May Day

May Day, an effective theatrical comedy unduly neglected since its initial run at the Blackfriars, appeared in the first years of the seventeenth century, probably in 1601 or 1602. Unlike *All*

Fools, this play is written almost entirely in prose. As in the case of *All Fools*, Chapman again borrowed a ready-made plot; but he transformed it, with his characteristic Elizabethan flair for comic action, into a drama far superior to the original. The source of *May Day* is the *Alessandro* of A. Piccolomini, an instance of the Italian *commedia erudita*, based on the Classic formulas of Plautus and Terence.[10] The *Alessandro* contained three separate plots, all of which Chapman retained. Central in the action was a serious love story in which the heroine, betrothed against her will to a wealthy old man, embarks on a secret assignation with a younger, more attractive suitor. A comic subplot concerned itself with the absurd attempts of a senile roué to arrange an affair with the wife of a *miles gloriosus*, and a romantic subplot complicates the whole affair through the conventional devices of disguise, mistaken identity, and long lost heirs.

Chapman succeeded in unifying these three disparate plots through introducing and expanding his favorite role, that of the intriguer, to manipulate and interweave the various threads of the action. The analogue to Lemot and Rinaldo in this play is Lodovico, who fulfills the same dramatic function but in a highly individualized characterization. The dominant trait of Lodovico is his energy, both physical and mental. His vigorous involvements are not at all, like those of Rinaldo, for the purpose of gulling susceptible victims, but rather to manifest his vitality, which must by its very nature exert itself in as many directions as possible. As Lodovico described himself in the usual device of the self-revealing soliloquy,

Idleness is accounted with other men a sin; to me 'tis a penance. I was begot in a stirring season, for now hath my soul a thousand fancies in an instant, as: what [a] wench dreams on when she lies on her back; when one hen lays an egg and another sits it, whether that hen shall mother that chicken; if my bull leap your cow, is not the calf yours? Yes, no doubt, for *Aedificium credit solo,* says the lawyer: and then to close all comes in a sentence, *Non omnia possimus omnes:* for some are born to riches, others to verses, some to be bachelors, others to be cuckolds, some to get crowns, and others to spend 'em, some to get children, and others to keep 'em: and all this is but idleness. Would to God I had some scurvy poem about me to laugh at! (III, iii, 136–148)

His own "scurvy" language exhibits racy, uninhibited Elizabethan prose, as when, for example, he taunts young Amelia
with a scathing verbal portrait of her aged suitor: "I'll tell thee
what he is—an old sapless trunk, fit to make touch-wood of, hollow and bald like a blasted oak, on whose top ravens sit and
croak the portents of funerals; one that noints his nose with
clouted cream and pomatum. His breath smells like the butt end
of a shoemaker's horn. A lep'rous scaly hide like an elephant" (II,
i, 64–70). He is so much a man of action that he restlessly scorns
his friend Aurelio's dawdling over pretty compliments while he
ascends the ladder to his mistress' bedroom, and, as he waits outside impatiently for his friend to complete the assignation, he is
quite ready to relieve his tedious vigil by following a bawd to an
appointment designed for another gallant!

With his propensity for doubling roles, Chapman also provided
two intriguers and two senile lovers. Lodovico shares his role as
intriguer with Angelo, who is less appealing than the ebullient,
madcap Lodovico. His gulling of Lorenzo, the aging gallant, car-
ries the sting of personal retribution. Like Lodovico, however,
Angelo is keen and imaginative, and his quick wits thrive on
crisis. In contrast to the sympathetic character of Lorenzo is the
clownish figure of the aged Gasparo, would-be betrothed to the
lovely heroine. Gasparo is the butt of everyone's satirical wit
whereas Lorenzo, trapped in his own folly, is never a mere dupe.
Lorenzo opens the play, with his January voice delivering a mock
eulogy to May, as he composes verses to Mistress Franchescina,
wife to old Captain Quintiliano. He enlists the aid of Angelo in
arranging a meeting with her at home in her husband's absence.
Angelo hits upon the far-fetched device of disguising Lorenzo
as the chimney-sweep Snail in order for him to gain entrance
secretly. Lorenzo seizes the suggestion blindly, never suspecting
that Angelo and Mistress "Frank" will conspire to mortify him
in his disabling disguise by locking him up in the coal house.

Chapman also incorporates his usual scholar-pedant contrast in
May Day in which the scholar is not the intriguer but the romantic hero, Aurelio. Early in the action this melancholy young man,
prostrated over the futility of his love for Amelia, is discovered
by Lodovico, who taunts his behavior as unworthy of a scholar:
"Is it not pity to see a man of good hope, a toward scholar,
writes a theme well, scans a verse very well, . . . And yet all

this overthrown as you see" (I, i, 198–99, 202–3). And the impetuous Lodovico must prod the eloquent but procrastinating
scholar to keep his amorous tryst: "Zounds, wilt thou melt into
rhyme o'the tother side? Shall we have lines? Change thy style
for a ladder; this will bring thee to Parnassus" (III, iii, 93–95).

In contrast to the affectionate mockery of the scholar is the
outright scorn reserved for the silly pedant, Giovanello, "A Fresh-
man come from Padua," (II, i, 537) "even now arrived . . . to
see fashions" (II, i, 627). Eager for dicing and wenching, as well
as for the latest fashion, this exemplar of false learning, who
ostentatiously parrots his "scientia" and "scientificus," is easily
gulled by the fluent, imaginative, and more genuinely, if not formally, learned Quintiliano.

A more complex figure than his prototype, the *miles gloriosus*
of the *Alessandro*, Quintiliano is one of the most convincing
characterizations in the play. Although he has the conventional
swagger of the braggart soldier—his "humour"—he also manifests the ready wit of the tavern companion, the cleverness of the
"cony-catcher" (swindler), and the hyperbole of a Falstaff. His
quick scorn disarms Giovanello at once: "S'blood, whose fool are
you? Are not you the tassel of a gander?" (II, i, 606–7). But, with
an eye to exacting five pounds from this promising victim, he introduces him to Lodovico as "an excellent scholar, a fine Cicero-
nian." He also gulls a natural victim, the guileless Innocentio,
into challenging the student to a duel: "my Lieutenant is in the
next chamber casting cold ink upon the flame of his courage to
keep him from the blot of cowardice" (III, iii, 257–59). And he
abuses poor disguised Lorenzo who has been exposed in his attempt to seduce the old captain's wife: "fetch me a coal-sack;
I'll put him in it, and hang him up for a sign" (IV, i, 84–85).

One of the theatrical features of *May Day* is its extensive parody of current stage hits. The scene in which Captain Quintiliano
gives detailed advice to Innocentio regarding proper behavior in
an ordinary (tavern) bears a close resemblance to a scene in Jonson's *Every Man Out of His Humour*. His brief drinking song
(IV, i, 18–19) mockingly echoes the tyrant's lines in Marston's
Antonio's Revenge. Innocentio's formal letter of challenge is comparable to that delivered to Sir Andrew Aguecheek in *Twelfth
Night*. Somewhat more subtle is Giovanello's application of a line
from *Hamlet*: "Come, be not retrograde to our desires." (III, iii,

196). The sorry pedant borrows the remark in a mood of levity in a tavern scene.

As well as the abundant parody, the inclusion of music, dance, and other elements of the masque contribute to the theatricality of the play. Extensive spectacle was also characteristic of performances at the Blackfriars, and the comedies which do not read particularly well were often much enlivened on the stage through this added dimension missing on the printed page. In *May Day* the long final scene would not have seemed drawn out (as it does to a reader) to a spectator with the visual benefit of the masque incorporated into the action. The functional use of the masque in the resolution of the action in this play is an intimation of Chapman's future interest in the stylized romance, with its organic incorporation of music and ritual.

One instance of sheer theatrical genius must always be mentioned in any discussion of *May Day*. A brilliant *coup de théâtre* that loses some effect in the reading occurs after Lodovico's wait for his friend Angelo to complete his assignation with Amelia, when, with his usual irrepressible vivacity, he has followed the bawd to a rendezvous intended for someone else. He follows her admonition to steal "gingerly" into Lucretia's room, where, as only the audience knows, lies the man Lucretio disguised in female attire. A few minutes later, Lodovico comes flying out, fighting for his life with drawn rapier, spitting blood and sputtering, "A plague of Gingerly!" (IV, ii, 151).

As a play rich in inherently comic situation, *May Day* is rarely surpassed, and its neglect by the theater since Chapman's time is hard to account for. Perhaps the topicality and parody interwoven into the texture of its language would inhibit the response of a contemporary audience, but surely less than that of *The Alchemist*, which has often succeeded. And, as in *The Alchemist*, the pungent prose is masterful. In any event, *May Day* is a worthy item in the comic repertoire of Chapman, and the last of those comedies structured on the principle of episodic display of "humour" character.

V Sir Giles Goosecap

Sir Giles Goosecap was entered anonymously in the Stationers Register on January 10, 1605–6, and later that year it was published anonymously in quarto form under the titular inscription:

Sir Gyles Goosecappe Knight. A Comedie presented by the Chil. of the Chapell. In spite of its anonymous appearance and its subsequent obscurity (it was not printed again until 1884), the play has been quite conclusively established as Chapman's. A. H. Bullen, editor of the 1884 edition, advanced Chapman's authorship on the basis of the similarity of certain passages to other scenes in Chapman's plays; and subsequent scholars have confirmed his speculations, thereby effectively closing the question of authorship.[11]

According to several dated allusions in the play, its composition must have been between the autumn of 1601 and the spring of 1603. For Chapman, the play was experimental; and it represents his waning interest in the comedy of "humours" and his growing attraction to romantic comedy. Hence the two plots of the play are more independent of each other than is usual in the dramatic construction of the era. The lingering popularity of "humour" comedy is evident in the fact that the titular figure is such a character, but the main plot of the play is wafted in on the new stream of romance.

The singularly static minor plot focuses on a conventional group of "humorous" figures. First to appear is Captain Foulweather, "a dull moist-brained ass" (I, i, 68), nicknamed Capt. Commendations because "he served the great Lady Kingcob and was yeoman of her wardrobe, and because 'a could brush up her silks lustily, she thought he would curry the enemies coasts as soundly, and so by her commendations he was made Captain in the Low Countries" (I, i, 74–78). Next in the parade is Sir Cuthbert Rudesby, "blunt at a sharp wit, and sharp at a blunt wit," "a good bustling gallant," and "two parts soldier" (I, i, 121–23). His "humour" is to say "emphatical," "with whose multiplicity often times he travails himself out of all good company" (I, i, 105–6). As for the third, the titular figure: "Sir Giles Goosecap has always a death's head (as it were) in his mouth, for his only one reason for everything is 'because we are all mortal'; and therefore he is generally called the mortal knight" (I, i, 110–13).

These three pompous fools are intent upon wooing widowed Countess Eugenia and two of her aristocratic lady friends, but their only achievement is to fall victim to a prank which sends them out on a cold mid-winter morning for a long, futile trip to a supposed trysting place. Having displayed their "humours" and demonstrated their infinite gullibility, the trio do little else in the play. Sir Giles supports his titular significance with a character somewhat more original than that of his stereotyped companions: he composes a foolish sonnet, excusing its illogic as *poetica licentia;* he admits to a "gentlewoman-like" skill with the needle; and he boasts such ingenious devices as kindling tobacco with glow worms which, although they work "better than all the burning-glasses i' th'world," (V, i, 65–66), are expensive to maintain—"I'll be sworn they eat me five faggots a week in charcoal" (V, i, 69–70). But even his whimsical eccentricities do not lift the subplot from the level of mere dialogue to that of dramatic action.

The serious plot commands more attention. In the romantic action, based on Chaucer's *Troilus and Criseyde,* the central situation of the play involves an analogous trio, the lovers and their go-between. In the mind of Chapman, however, the characters of all three have undergone a complete metamorphosis: the knight has become a scholar; the virgin, an aloof widow; and the uncle, a gentleman. Indeed, Eugenia, Chapman's heroine, represents an entirely different conception of womanhood from Chaucer's complexly feminine Criseyde. Eugenia is "a good learned scholar" and, as one editor put it, "a bit of a bluestocking." [12] But Chapman, who always defended learning in women, is not consciously mocking her. He praises her through her Uncle Momford: "learning in a woman is like weight in gold, or lustre in diamonds, which in no other stone is so rich or refulgent" (II, i, 51–53). She is also witty and charming although her extended period of mourning for her husband inhibits her social life. Momford affectionately gibes, "Why, alas, niece, y'are so smeared with this wilful-widow's-three-years black weed, that I never come to you but I dream of corses and sepulchres and epitaphs all the night after" (II, i, 56–59).

But for all her vaunted scholarship, Eugenia can be exceedingly worldly in her judgments. When Momford proposes a match with his poor young friend Clarence, a mere scholar unendowed with worldly goods, her objections to such a union are anything but philosophical. First, she fears public opinion—"the judgment of the world"—and then she scorns the prospect of poverty, mocking a worthless intellectual nobility which "will not maintain him a week. Such kind of nobleness gives no coats of honor, nor can scarce get a coat for necessity" (II, i, 186–187). Yet, when the moment of final decision comes, Eugenia beats her uncle to the draw, so to speak, by entering Clarence's sickroom to volunteer the medicine of her love while Momford is still plotting by devious means to entice her there. Her address to Clarence is aimed at the young man's Platonic spirit:

> Knowledge is the bond,
> The seal, and crown of our united minds,
> And that is rare and constant, and for that
> To my late written hand I give thee this.
> See, Heaven, the soul thou gav'st is in this hand;
> This is the knot of our eternity,
> Which Fortune, Death, nor Hell, shall ever loose. (V, ii, 215–21)

Eugenia is—at least by intention—an idealized portrait of a fine, formidably educated lady, but more touches of warmth and humor are needed to make her completely convincing.

Momford is even more different from Pandarus, his prototype, than Eugenia is from hers. Like Eugenia, he is aristocratic and learned; unlike her, he has an earthy frankness and easy friendliness which make him not only more convincing but also more likable. A sincerely devoted friend to young Clarence, he offers him an older man's advice about women: "Audacity prospers above probability in all worldly matters." And he buckles down to the hard task of winning Eugenia for him, resorting to trickery if necessary. Momford can fence with her using her own weapon of scholarship, and parrying her every Latin thrust. When erudition fails, trickery steps in. Supposedly writing a letter to Clarence at Eugenia's dictation, he inserts suggestive phrases of his own invention—an idea Chapman borrowed from Chaucer, enhancing it with his usual gift for comic situation. In the original poem Pandarus only offered to write, at Criseyde's dictation, a reply to Troilus' love letter; but Criseyde did not permit him to do so. Chapman heightened the comic possibilities of the situation by interweaving the equivocal words of Momford in the austere reply of Eugenia. But in the end Momford proves a generous uncle, as well as friend, by making Clarence "sole heir to all my earldom" when he weds Eugenia. And it is the jovial Momford who speaks the ritualistic *plaudite* at the end:

Now we will consecrate our ready supper
To honour'd Hymen at his nuptial rite;
In form whereof first dance, fair lords and ladies,
And after sing, so we will sing and dance,
And to the skies our virtuous joys advance.

Like the other principals, Clarence is entirely different from
his Chaucerian original. The sentimental knight Troilus has become a Platonic intellectual, an idealized figure and the most
complete portrayal of a scholar in any of Chapman's plays. Furthermore, since most of Clarence's ideas reflect those of his creator, it is tempting to see in this romantic hero a dramatic self-
portrait of George Chapman. Clarence first appears in a state of
melancholy over his love for Eugenia, and his perturbation is
prefaced by a comment on life itself as "a spring of vanities."
Although the scholarly melancholy and disdain of worldliness are
conventional, Clarence is also a rather esoteric scholar in a manner that recalls the "school of night," with his ultimate questions
about dark origins: "What soul the world's soul is, what the black
springs / And unreveal'd original of things, / What their perse-
verance, what is life and death, / And what our certain restaura-
tion." (II, i, 11–14).

Like Chapman, Clarence is talented in music, as well as philosophy, and cites Platonic explanation of its mystical value:
"According to my master Plato's mind / The soul is music, and
doth therefore joy / In accents musical." (III, ii, 2–4). As he
writes his letter to his beloved, the singer Horatio interpolates
music, while Eugenia herself becomes a veritable Platonic Idea
of Music: "Divine Eugenia bears the ocular form / Of music and
of Reason, and presents / The soul exempt from flesh in flesh
inflam'd; / Who must not love her then that loves his soul?" (III,
ii, 7–10). The harmony of their love seems to echo the music of
the spheres.

Clarence also resembles Hamlet, although somewhat less than
his predecessor Dowsecer. Like the moody Dane, Clarence speculates sardonically on the married life:

I marry, and bid states, and entertain
Ladies with tales and jests, and lords with news
And keep a house to feed Actaeon's hounds
That eat their master, and let idle guests

> Draw me from serious search of things divine
> To bid them sit and welcome, and take care
> To soothe their palates with choice kitchen stuff,
> As all must do that marry and keep house! (III, ii, 40–46)

His complaints about the rank state of the world focus more on
the private weeds of his personal garden than on the general
corruption which dismayed Hamlet:

> 'Twixt whom and me, and every worldly fortune,
> There fights such sour and curst antipathy,
> So waspish and so petulant a star,
> That all things tending to my grace or good
> Are ravish'd from their object, as I were
> A thing created for a wilderness. (I, iv, 46–51)

But Clarence is a hero with intimations: his quarrel with Fortune,
his learning, and his philosophy will reappear in a stronger *per-
sona* in the tragedy to come. As for the play which is his vehicle,
Sir Giles Goosecap is more interesting for its transitional features
than for its intrinsic worth. It tolls the death knell of "humour"
comedy and rings in the tragicomedy of romance.

CHAPTER 4

More Matter Than Mirth

THE turn of the seventeenth century was also a turning point in Chapman's career as a writer of stage comedies. After *Sir Giles Goosecap* he abandoned the comedy of "humours" altogether in favor of experimentation in the new type of comedy already hinted at in the Eugenia-Clarence plot. With the appearance of *The Gentleman Usher* (printed in 1606 but probably written and performed as early as 1602), Chapman introduced to the English stage the new genre later to flourish under the fluent pens of Beaumont and Fletcher: the romantic tragicomedy. Although this new form was refined by the lighthanded, cavalier touch of these poets, Chapman deserves credit both for the innovation and for two masterful specimens of it, *The Gentleman Usher* and *Monsieur d'Olive*.

The fundamental feature of Jacobean tragicomedy[1] is the mingling of tragic and comic elements rather than that sharp juxtaposition characteristic of the earlier, Elizabethan drama. The gay and somber tones are subtly blended; the amusing and the threatening episodes are no longer contrapuntal but virtually indistinguishable. Frequently, in this blurring of the traditional polarities of mood, the absolutes of good and evil also commingle so as to lose all clear distinction. The dynamic Elizabethan confrontation of moral opposites fades into a world devoid of value judgments in which the virtuous surrender to unworthy passions and in which the villainous are dismissed rather than punished. In the absence of clearcut moral conflict, characterization often becomes dissipated and a sense of unreality ensues. In such plays, the central event of the plot, usually involving romantic love, is supplemented by episodes of exaggerated, even fanciful, adventure. The setting of the romantic action is unrealistic, usually a foreign principality, sometimes a never-never land. With theme and characterization subordinate to the mise-en-scène, probability is neglected in favor of stage effects directed toward achieving a melo-dramatic impact; and plot is manipulated ruthlessly through unexpected reversals, surprise intrusions, contrived suspense, and sudden denouement effected by a deus ex machina. Unnatural-istic in its basic conventions, the tragicomedy is self-consciously theatrical. Plays-within-a-play are frequent, as are formal rituals and elaborate masques. The artificiality of the form is often en-hanced by interpolations of music and dance that convert these plays into spectacles of the lavish Broadway variety. Unfortu-nately, the absence of visual appeal conferred by performance often frustrates the mere reader of these plays.

Although Chapman's two tragicomedies conform to this de-scription in a general way, they also display notable differences. Chapman was too much of a rigid moralist of the old school to submit to decadence or laxity; therefore, the ethical values of his plays are not blurred. The moral tone of *The Gentleman Usher* is, in fact, elevated even beyond that of most of Chapman's come-dies. His characterization is also considerably stronger: here ap-pear some of Chapman's most memorable individual portraits. Finally, although the atmosphere of unreality exists, it is not per-vasive but carefully juxtaposed with the concrete realities. But after his promising excursion into tragicomedy, Chapman re-turned to the realistic local scene and to the mode of satire for his two last comedies. *Eastward Ho*, written in collaboration with Jonson and Marston, is a realistic comedy of London life; and *The Widow's Tears* is a bitter satire poised mockingly on the edge of tragedy.

I The Gentleman Usher

Although no record of its stage career exists, *The Gentleman Usher* was printed with elaborate stage directions, indicative of performance in the highly theatrical and stylized manner of the Children of the Chapel. Probably acted by this group in 1601 or 1602, this play is not only a highly successful example of tragi-comedy but, from the viewpoint of dramatic structure and coher-ence, one of the best plays that Chapman ever wrote. Although the action gets off to a slow start in the first two acts, the move-ment of the last three acts is handled with skill and control. In the play's heightened moral perspective, it transcends the limita-tions of its genre, inclining toward tragic intensity; and, as much as any other single work of its author, it is philosophically concerned with the reality of virtue and with the fraudulent illusoriness of vice.

In the main plot, the heroine, Margaret, resists the advances of the Duke Alphonso because of her love for the Duke's son, Vincentio. The young lovers, unable to be married publicly because of the Duke's rivalry, swear oaths of fidelity in a private marriage ceremony. The gentleman-usher Bassiola feels exalted in his role of go-between in this romantic intrigue. In the subplot, Strozza, friend and confidant of the hero, is primarily concerned in saving the Duke from his dangerous and unworthy favorite, Medice, who poses a threat to Vincentio's royal heritage. Both plots approach a tragic crisis: Margaret disfigures herself to escape a forced marriage, and Strozza is seriously wounded through the villainy of Medice. But in the last act, both Margaret and Strozza are miraculously cured; the lovers united; and Medice banished.

The heterogeneous elements of this tragicomic plot derive from a number of sources, but some of the characters, as well as some of the episodes, are original with Chapman. The central plot situation—the rivalry in love of a father and son—is, of course, an old stage tradition. Chapman would have known it from several of Plautus' plays and might have seen it in the anonymous play *The Wisdom of Dr. Dodypoll,* in which the father's name is also Alphonso. The sensational episode of the heroine's self-disfigurement had appeared in literature as early as *The Heptameron* (Marguerite of Navarre), but Chapman's most likely familiarity with it would have been either from Sir Philip Sidney's *Arcadia*[2] or from William Painter's *Palace of Pleasure,*[3] both of which Chapman refers to inaccurately in the play.[4] In addition to outside sources for specific episodes, Chapman resorted frequently to borrowing from his own recent play *Sir Giles Goosecap.* The low comic character of the foolish Poggio is obviously a recasting of Sir Giles (indeed, he is called so in the play); Cortezza fulfills the abortive role of the drunken Lady Furnivall in the previous play; and the letter-writing scene is transplanted, with considerable gain, to the titular figure of Bassiolo. The major-domo himself may have been created in part as a take-off on Shakespeare's Malvolio; but, if so, he is sufficiently distinctive to leave his prototype a safe distance behind. The remainder of the play, including the impressive figure of the noble courtier Strozza, is entirely original.

Chapman followed his usual propensity for doubling and paralleling roles in this play, even in respect to women on whom, as a rule, he did not lavish much textual attention. A triple study in analogy, the three main female roles in the play are those of a maiden, a matron, and a crone. The first two are idealized; the last, satirized. The maiden Margaret, the heroine, first appears engaged in an elaborate masque (Act I) staged for her benefit by Duke Alphonso, who hopes to win her in marriage. As she is secretly in love with Alphonso's son Vincent, she resists the seductive implications of the pageant tactfully but firmly by recalling its fundamental fantasy. When, in the course of the masque, she is called upon to unbind the captive Duke, she concedes with a sharp reminder of reality: "If it were serious; but it is sport" (I, ii, 127). And, in the second masque scene (Act II), when Alphonso begs her to mount his throne, she reminds him again to "not make serious scruple of a toy" (II, i, 188). In her firm sense of reality, as in her courage and charm, Margaret suggests the late heroines of Shakespearean romance, Imogen in particular. Although not so witty as Shakespeare's Portia or Rosalind, she has their same spirited sense of fun and gulls the gentleman-usher with imaginative zest; and, if not so poetical as Juliet or Desdemona, she exchanges spiritual marriage vows with her betrothed in a high flight of pure lyricism. When Margaret later receives the false news that her lover has been slain, she is distraught with grief; and, unable to take her own life, she instead destroys her beauty by applying to her face a vicious ointment procured from her Aunt Cortezza. When the wounded Vincentio is returned to her, she nobly refuses to inflict her ugly self upon him. But beauty and virtue triumph: a miraculous cure is suddenly offered by the doctor, and the lovers are restored to each other.

As Margaret is the high-minded young virgin, Cynanche is the noble, devoted matron. When she first appears in the play, she is apprehensive about a boar hunt in which her husband Strozza is soon to take part. Her intuition proves prophetic: he receives a nearly fatal wound, but not from the boar as she had feared. Human malice is even more bestial. When Cynanche learns of the wound inflicted by an arrow, her first thought is for her husband, not herself: "I dare not yield to grief, / But force feign'd patience to recomfort him" (IV, i, 11–12). When Strozza in the agony of pain cries out for a means of suicide, Cynanche restrains him, appealing to the fortitude of his higher nature: "Patience in torment is a valour more / Than ever crown'd th'Alcmenean conqueror" (IV, i, 56–57). The loving wife's wisdom and patience eventually comfort and calm her husband who delivers an eloquent eulogy to her as an ideal wife:

> Oh, what a treasure is a virtuous wife,
> Discreet and loving! Not one gift on earth
> Makes a man's life so highly bound to heaven;
> She gives him double forces, to endure
> And to enjoy, by being one with him,
> Feeling his joys and griefs with equal sense. (IV, iii, 11–16)

Hers is also the voice of Christianity in the play, and she later persuades Strozza to make a religious vow and pilgrimage in gratitude for his miraculous survival.

Whereas Margaret and Cynanche exemplify two phases of ideal womanhood, the vulgar Cortezza, sister of Margaret's father Lasso, embodies the opposite extreme. The maiden and the matron are both spiritual and high-minded, but the old crone is animalistic and crude. A drunkard, she responds to alcohol by making amorous advances to the Duke's minion: "[She] does nothing but kiss my lord Medice," (III, ii, 231) and she grotesquely exhibits her bulging leg—"a good leg still, still a good calf, and not [f]labby, nor hanging, I warrant you" (III, ii, 237–39). Her drunkenness is excused by Lasso as a mere "humour," but in this play in which moral values are real, Cortezza's drinking becomes a symbol of her depraved, spiritually starved nature. It is she who urges Margaret to accept the elderly Duke for the sake of acquiring his wealth and title, and it is she who stupidly, if not in fact maliciously, suggests to Margaret that she disfigure her face with the vile ointment. Cortezza appropriately disappears from the final scene of reconciliation and recovery so as not to disturb the harmony of the romantic denouement. Between the crude Cortezza and the noble Margaret and Cynanche lies the whole world of womankind.

The male roles in *The Gentleman Usher* are also clearly and effectively drawn. Vincentio is a creditable romantic hero who

proves his physical bravery by risking his life for his beloved and
by asserting his spiritual energy in defying the double authority
of his ducal parent. That he also possesses wit and imagination
is shown in the scenes in which he gulls the usher Bassiola into
becoming the go-between in his secret romance. And his language
is richly poetic, as when he conceives his spiritual marriage vow:

> here I vow by heaven,
> By the most sweet imaginary joys
> Of untried nuptials, by Love's ushering fire
> Fore-melting beauty, and Love's flame itself,
> As this is soft and pliant to your arm
> In a circumferent flexure, so will I
> Be tender of your welfare and your will
> As of mine own, as of my life and soul,
> In all things, and for ever. (IV, ii, 155–63)

He also proves that he is no superficial lover smitten with his
bride's mere beauty, for he insists when she mars her lovely physiognomy—"I won your virtues, which as I am sure / No accident
can alter or impair, / So, be you certain, nought can change my
love" (V, iv, 97–99). But, although Vincentio is a likeable enough
protagonist, he is somewhat overshadowed by several other
strong male characterizations, especially those of Strozza and
Bassiola.

Strozza—actually a second hero in the play—needs to be
viewed in the context of Chapman's gallery of scholars. Strozza
represents the philosophical man whose "learning the art is of
good life," but three other roles in this play embody the negation
of true learning. Medice, in reality Mendice, is a pretender, an
exemplar of fraudulent learning; Sarpego, a pedant, of acquired
ignorance; Poggio, a fool, of natural ignorance. Strozza, like
Clarence before him and the tragic Clermont after him, acts as
spokesman of his author's ideas. A frank and outspoken man, he
condemns the tyranny of the Duke to his face, voicing a favorite
Chapmanesque idea developed in the tragedies: "Had all been
virtuous men, / There never had been prince upon the earth" (V,
iv, 56–57). He bluntly states his dislike of "that fustian lord," the
Duke's unworthy minion, Medice: "I would have such a noble
counterfeit nail'd / Upon the pillory, and, after, whipp'd / For his
adultery with nobility" (I, i, 121–24).

But, although Strozza is presented initially as an admirable stoic figure, he is even more ennobled when he is felled by an arrow shot upon Medice's malevolent orders. At first the pain is so great he calls for death:

> Must we attend at Death's abhorred door
> The torturing delays of slavish Nature?
> My life is in mine own powers to dissolve:
> And why not then the pains that plague my life? (IV, i, 35–38)

But this stoical decision, based on "manliest reason," gives way to something higher—Christian mysticism. When Strozza transcends the excruciating pain, he achieves an almost superhuman victory over suffering and becomes so spiritualized by the experience that he gains power of prophecy:

> Humility hath rais'd me to the stars;
> In which (as in a sort of crystal globes)
> I sit and see things hid from human sight.
> Ay, even the very accidents to come
> Are present with my knowledge; the seventh day
> The arrow-head will fall out of my side. (IV, iii, 61–66)

Hereafter he will teach the physician "To build his c[u]res hereafter upon Heaven / More than on earthly med'cines" (IV, iii, 72–73). And, in the final scene as he confronts the repentant Duke, Strozza again voices an idea echoed in the tragedies: "A virtuous man is subject to no prince, / But to his soul and honour" (V, iv, 59–60).

Arranged in dramaturgic contrast to Strozza are the three already mentioned exemplars of false learning. Medice, the villain of the piece, is a counterfeit who does not even know how to dress as a true nobleman and who is ludicrously inept when it comes his turn to improvise lines in the masque. Alphonso must ask Strozza to take over the part and discharge his speech for him, a procedure which leaves the audience wondering what the Duke sees in this manifestly unworthy man. Medice admits his own contempt for "book learning," and his preference for "practical," empirical knowledge, scoffing at educated men like Strozza and Vincentio:

> They stand upon their wits and paper-learning;
> Give me a fellow with a natural wit
> That can make wit of no wit; and wade through
> Great things with nothing, when their wits stick fast. (II, i, 58–60)

This alignment of attitudes recalls the School of Night controversy between the formally trained artist and the intuitive "villanest" who learns from his wits and his immediate experience.[5]

Even Bassiolo despises "that Bobadilio, / That foolish knave, that hose and doublet stinkard" (V, i, 55–56); but it is the profoundly honest Strozza who finally exposes the fraudulent pose of Medice. He reveals that semblance of "noblesse" to be entirely a reflection of the Duke's misguided favor:

> Set by your princely favour,
> That gave the lustre to his painted state,
> Who ever view'd him but with deep contempt,
> As reading vileness in his very looks?
> And if he prove not son of some base drudge,
> Trimm'd up by Fortune, . . .
> . . . I'll confess I do him open wrong. (V, iv, 194–199, 205)

Medice finally confesses his own vagabond past. Far from being the titled aristocrat he claimed, he is a man without even a country, born on the seas, as his mother was passing "twixt Zant and Venice." [6] As a youth he was adopted and reared by a band of gipsies until he decided to seek his fortune by feigning nobility at court. The pretender is ousted in disgrace and driven into banishment, disguised.

Sarpego and Poggio also represent perversions of proper learning. Sarpego is the overeducated pedant. Like the traditional stock figure of the stage pedant, he interpolates Latin into virtually every remark but cannot understand the simplest word. Even the nightcap he is to wear in the masque baffles his understanding; "I do *ignorare* / How I should wear it" (II, i, 127–28). Poggio, on the other hand, is the simpleton lacking equally in formal education and in native mother wit. Like his prototype Sir Giles Goosecap, he repeatedly reverses the word order of his sentences so that his Uncle Strozza calls him "Hysteron Proteron." Delighted with his role as Broom-man in the masque, Poggio reads his bad verses with proud zest.

The titular figure of Bassiolo offers still another perspective on the theme of learning. The gentleman-usher is rich in knowledge —of his own superiority. A mere major-domo, he is inflated with a self-conceit that exalts his sense of his own importance beyond all discretion. When Vincentio, the young nobleman, offers him the compliment of his friendship, Bassiolo immediately accepts his equality with "Vince" and brashly behaves with excessive intimacy. And when Margaret asks his aid in penning a love letter, he is too confident of his prowess to recognize that she is mocking him. Bassiolo bears some resemblance to Shakespeare's Malvolio in his general function as major-domo in the plot and in his comic role as gull. But, although he may well have been modeled on that classic "precisionist," he is no patent imitation. Bassiolo's temperament is not at all that of the stiff-necked Puritan, and his ingratiating personality makes him vulnerable to teasing, not tormenting: there is no dislike on the part of those who so amiably gull him. In fact, his charm triumphs over his vanity; as Professor Parrott has so neatly put it, "Malvolio is a grim peacock, Bassiolo is a good-natured goose." [7] Providing dramaturgic contrast to the egotistic Bassiolo is the minor but clearly drawn figure of the doctor Benevemus. He is the quiet, capable servant who quite without ostentation provides at the moment of crisis a miraculous cure. He functions in the realm of action but the gentleman-usher flourishes in the illusory realm of vain words and heady dreams.

As the characters are stylized in their balance and parallelism in this play, so the structure of *The Gentleman Usher* incorporates a ritualistic stylization.[8] Spectacle is not merely gratuitous but functions as ritual, both advancing and illuminating the plot. The first two acts present a masque and countermasque: the first is contrived by Alphonso to win the approval of Margaret; and the second, a return gesture staged by her father Count Lasso. The amorous Duke presents himself as bound by an Enchanter, to be freed only by the mercy of Margaret. Count Lasso, in his turn, offers a pastoral complete with a man Bug and a lady Bug. Written by the pedantic Sarpego, this playlet is actually complementary to the Duke's show: the pastoral in its sing-song fashion scorns "the fault of Virgin nicety" and clumsily advises Margaret: "Yet take you in your ivory clutches / This noble Duke, and be his Duchess" (II, i, 296–97).

Act III involves a comic ritual: Vincentio's induction of Bassi-olo into grotesque intimacy is followed by Margaret's mock per-suasion of the gullible usher to indite a pompous love letter. In Act IV the private and profound ritual of marriage is solemnly performed when the young lovers, unable to wed lawfully, ex-change vows of eternal fidelity. Meanwhile, a ritual action of a very different sort—the boar hunt—has taken place, with the malicious attack on Strozza by Medice's hireling and the sub-sequent miraculous cure by nature, prophesied by the inspired victim. In Act V, the ritual reconciliation of all conflicts is achieved through an analogous wound and cure: the disfigure-ment of Margaret and her restoration by means of a miraculous mask. Strozza simultaneously announces his projected walk to Rome to deposit the arrowhead as a sacred relic—"which work let none judge / A superstitious rite, but a right use, / Proper to this peculiar instrument" (V, iii, 36–38). And conversely, the oust-ing of Medice—the counterfeit, the "unclean" member of the com-munity, the human arrowhead threatening the vitals of the young lovers—is analogous to the expulsion of the mortal arrow from the flesh of Strozza.

Ritualistic and stylized, patterned with parallel characters and episodes, *The Gentleman Usher* does not in any way suffer from artificiality. An excellent and uniformly entertaining play, it is enhanced by artifice. Its varied characterizations are convincing; and its action, delicately poised between naturalistic and fanciful, avoids both the extremes of melodrama and sentimentality. Both character and action are enriched by the thematic conflict of reality and illusion. It is a serious play without being heavy; comic, without being flippant. And in this play Chapman has reached mastery of blank verse. The dialogue moves with easy fluency, and with graceful modulations between the elevated and the frivolous. Controlled and flexible, the poetry functions artfully as dramatic medium. The play is not only a worthy in-troduction to the tragicomic romance, but it also transcends many of its successors in the genre.

II Monsieur d'Olive

Chapman never recaptured the harmonious tone of *The Gentle-man Usher*. Although *Monsieur d'Olive* is an exceptionally enter-taining play, it is weakened by a basically incoherent dramatic structure. Like its predecessor, it has two plots, one romantic and one comic, but the connection between them is mechanical rather than organic. Each act has two scenes, one on each level of action; only occasionally are the two lines contrapuntal; never are they fused.

Published in 1606, *Monsieur d'Olive* was staged about 1604–05 according to internal evidence, for the subplot has its source in the contemporary scene. The ambassage theme was a lively one in the early years of James' rule when ambassadors sprung up in notorious abundance. The sources of the double romantic plot, on the other hand, are legendary and traditional. One line of action—the retirement of Marcellina from the world because of her husband's jealousy—is founded in the Courtly Love cult which flourished in an earlier century. The other—the refusal of the grieved St. Anne to bury the body of his wife—has many legendary prototypes, including Herod and Miriamne, and Charlemagne and his queen.[9]

Swinburne praised the "overture" or exposition of this play as "one of the most admirable" opening scenes in all drama—and his tribute is not extravagant. As the play opens, the central figure of Vandome appears before the house of his old friend Count Vaumont, where he has just arrived after a three year absence abroad. The young man delivers a philosophical soliloquy in which he expresses in erudite language his Platonic love for his courtly mistress, Marcellina, wife of Vaumont. But his eager approach to the house becomes ominous, for the gates are shut and deserted, tapers burn within curtained windows at midday, and the Count, who paces strangely before the door, coldly retreats from his friend's advances. Vandome then learns from him of the double catastrophe befallen during his absence: Marcellina has retired from the world, pledged to live hereafter in darkness because of her husband's jealousy of Vandome; even worse, Vandome's sister has died, and her grief-stricken husband refuses to bury her body but retains her corpse treated with "restoring balms." A most promising, albeit melodramatic, opening scene.

Unfortunately, the remainder of the play does not fulfill the expectations of this highly dynamic beginning. Vandome undertakes to amend the grim situation by manipulation. First, he wins the affection of St. Anne, a feat of diplomacy made easier by his resemblance to his dead sister. Then he engages St. Anne in an intrigue designed to make the widower fall in love with Eurione, close friend of Marcellina. Vandome's plot is an instant success, much to the astonishment of the newly smitten St. Anne, who promptly buries his dead wife. Vandome then turns his attention to his immured mistress, Marcellina. He entices her from her self-inflicted solitude by falsely informing her that her husband, during her absence, is having an affair with another woman. When Vandome cheerfully admits his double conspiracy, both couples are reconciled. In the meantime, the would-be ambassador, Monsieur d'Olive, is compensated for the loss of his mission by being rescued from the numerous hangers-on who had attached themselves to him in the hope of joining the elegant ambassage. The suggestive situations introduced in the main plot are too readily resolved, and the boldly sketched characters dwindle into types. The grief-stricken husband, the Earl of St. Anne, is introduced as both an idealistic and an idealized figure:

> at her feet
> He, like a mortified hermit clad,
> Sits weeping out his life, as having lost
> All his life's comfort;
> . . . .
> But to lift all his thoughts
> Up to another world where she expects him,
> He feeds his ears with soul-exciting music,
> Solemn and tragical, and so resolves
> In those sad accents to exhale his soul. (I, i, 160–163, 169–173)

He is philosophical, even scholarly, in his defense of this extreme behavior. In a conversation with Vandome, one in which Chapman draws heavily on Petrarch's *Secretum*,[10] St. Anne describes his profound melancholy:

> I feel in these deep griefs, to which I yield
> (A kind of false, sluggish, and rotting sweetness
> Mix'd with an humour where all things in life
> Lie drown'd in sour, wretched, and horrid thoughts)
> The way to cowardly desperation opened;
> And whatsoever urgeth souls accurs'd
> To their destruction, and sometimes their plague,
> So violently gripes me, that I lie

Whole days and nights bound at his tyrannous feet;
So that my days are not like life or light,
But bitterest death, and a continual night. (III, i, 8–19)

But St. Anne does not sustain the promising introduction to his role. He is all too easily persuaded to leave his gloomy chamber by Vandome, who perpetrates a ruse to introduce his friend to the lovely Eurione, whose physical resemblance to the dead wife stirs the passion that he had thought also dead. But his change of heart is all too abrupt, and St. Anne loses interest for the reader.

Vandome, the central figure in the action of the play, also degenerates in characterization as the play progresses. From his initial appearance as a dashing lover-scholar-adventurer, he fades into a mere intriguer, a plot manipulator. At first a learned cosmopolitan gentleman who discourses of his mistress in neo-Platonic language and debates with her husband in Petrarchan arguments, he is suddenly reduced to a kind of gadfly, flitting about to unite St. Anne and Eurione, and to extricate Marcellina from her self-inflicted night. He moves from the individualized, internalized protagonist of the opening act to the conventionally objectified and externalized agent whose main function is to tie together the two disparate strands of the romantic plot. He is in a strategic position to do so by virtue of his relationship both to the unburied wife, his sister, and to the "buried" wife, his mistress.

The female roles are pallid. Marcellina, the injured lady who perverts day to night, is sketchily drawn. She never rises above the almost allegorical pose of offended dignity that drives her into the depths to escape the thorny world of suspicion. Although the pages Roderigue and Mugeron joke cynically about the supposedly Platonic devotion of Vandome to his "mistress," there is no suggestion of sensuality to mar their deeply innocent devotion to each other. As for Eurione, who shares her self-imposed entombment, she comes to life momentarily in the scene in which Vandome lures her from her vault by arousing her anger against the "blabber-lipp'd blouse" who supposedly is playing false with Vaumont.

The subplot, paralleling but not intersecting the main plot, is focused on the planned ambassage of the gay, foppish, conceited d'Olive. Because of his quick wit and imaginative gift of language, he is what his friends call "the compound of a poet and a lawyer."

He fancies himself a bit of a scholar: "I will have my chamber the rendezvous of all good wits, the shop of good words, the mint of good jests, an ordinary of fine discourse; critics, essayists, linguists, poets, and other professors of that faculty of wit, shall at certain hours i'th'day resort thither; it shall be a second Sorbonne, where all doubts or differences of learning, honour, duellism, criticism, and poetry shall be disputed" (I, i, 300–8).

But d'Olive's conceit makes him vulnerable to gulling; and, when his friends Roderigue and Mugeron learn that the Duke, uncle to the dead countess, plans to send someone to entreat her husband to give her a proper burial, they conspire to persuade d'Olive to apply for the ambassage. Recommended for this particular mission, d'Olive jauntily appears before the Duke to whom he at first presents himself as a recluse whose "mind is his kingdom." But he asserts himself verbally, becoming ever more eloquent and presumptuously forward. When he rises to lyrical heights on the subject of tobacco, his eulogy to the "profane weed" is a minor masterpiece of Elizabethan prose.

Tobacco, that excellent plant, the use whereof (as of fift element) the world cannot want, is that little shop of Nature, wherein her whole workmanship is abridged, where you may see earth kindled into fire, the fire breathe out an exhalation which, ent'ring in at the mouth, walks through the regions of a man's brain, drives out all ill vapours but itself, draws down all bad humours by the mouth, which in time might breed a scab over the whole body, if already they have not: a plant of singular use; for, on the one side, Nature being an enemy to vacuity and emptiness, and, on the other, there being so many empty brains in the world as there are, how shall Nature's course be continued? How shall these empty brains be filled but with air, Nature's immediate instrument to that purpose? If with air, what so proper as your fume? What fume so healthful as your perfume? What perfume so sovereign as tobacco? Besides the excellent edge it gives a man's wit (as they can best judge that have been present at a feast of tobacco, where commonly all good wits are consorted) what variety of discourse it begets, what sparks of wit it yields, it is a world to hear! As likewise to the courage of a man; for if it be true that Johannes [Savonarola] writes, that he that drinks verjuice pisseth vinegar, then it must needs follow to be as true, that he that eats smoke farts fire. For garlic I will not say, because it is a plant of our own country, but it may cure the diseases of the country; but for the diseases of the Court, they are out of the element of garlic to medicine. To conclude, as there is no enemy to tobacco but garlic, so there is no friend to garlic but a sheep's head; and so I conclude. (II, ii, 252–81)

Giddy with this verbal triumph, he presumes too far; and, departing with a flourish, he kisses the Duchess Jacqueline. Despite her obvious consternation, he feels himself a great success at court; and his sense of the importance of the projected ambassage becomes even more inflated: "men shall reckon their years, women their marriages, from the day of our ambassage; as 'I was born, or married, two, three, or four years before the great ambassage.' Farmers shall count their leases from this day; gentlemen their mortgages from this day; St. Denis shall be raced out of the calendar, and the day of our instalment entered in red letters; and as St. Valentine's day is fortunate to choose lovers, St. Luke's to choose husbands, so shall this day be to the choosing of lords" (IV, ii, 113–22).

But, after the grandiose preparations and the accumulation of followers, news comes suddenly that the voyage is "dashed": the lady is entombed; the mission is buried. Unhappily, it is only the third act. Roderigue acknowledges the theatrical problem: "Here we may strike the Plaudite to our play; my lord Fool's gone; all our audience will forsake us." But he and Mugeron, as if in a desperate attempt to keep the play going, gull d'Olive with a fake love-letter from a lady at court, a flat device that is anti-climactical to the ambassage. The disappointed "ambassador" is treated graciously—although he is relieved of his post—by the Duke, who promises to secure him from the large rabble of followers who still plague him as hangers-on, not knowing that the mission has been cancelled.

Unfortunately, no real interaction occurs between Monsieur d'Olive and the principals in the main plot. The resolution of the double plot is entirely external. The parallel plot lines meet only momentarily as a result of Vandome's match-making manipulations. In fact, when Vandome succeeds in uniting St. Anne and Eurione in the final scene of the play, he encounters for the first time the titular figure whose ambassadorial mission he has unwittingly obliterated. The failure of the two hemispheres of action to unite not only disrupts the harmony of the play but also confines the ingratiating charm of the titular character to a small canvas. The play as a whole, however, is highly entertaining in its dialogue—which ranges from the lyrical beauty of the verse spoken by the lovers to the vigorous, racy prose of the subplot—as well as memorable for its portrait of the glib, dapper, fluent "ambassador," one of the most original comic figures of the Jacobean stage.

III Eastward Ho

Eastward Ho, the only comedy known to have been written by Chapman in collaboration with other playwrights,[11] appeared at the Blackfriars in 1605. It was conceived to compete with *Westward Ho,* the highly successful play of Dekker and Webster performed by the rival company at St. Paul's, since the prologue admits as much in its coy denial: "Not out of envy, for there's no effect, / Where there's no cause; nor out of imitation, / For we have evermore been imitated" (ll. 1–3). *Westward Ho* had inaugurated a new theatrical vogue, the realistic comedy of London life, a fashion which continued to be exploited by such writers as Dekker and Middleton throughout the next decade. *Eastward Ho,* the first such city comedy to appear at the Blackfriars, was distinguished from the other popular specimens of the genre by its strong conventional morality—an inevitable feature issuing from the common didactic bias of its three authors, Jonson, Marston, and Chapman.

The old-fashioned main plot follows the homiletic outline of a morality play. The honest and industrious goldsmith Touchstone has two contrasting apprentices: Golding, a model of industry, thrift, and propriety; Quicksilver, a debauched and unprincipled gallant. Touchstone also has two daughters, equally opposed in temperament and character. Mildred, also a model of virtue, naturally marries Golding; Gertrude, a rude upstart with pretensions to a title, falls victim to her own mercenary ambitions by marrying a fraudulent aristocrat, Sir Petronel Flash, who is actually a confidence man out to rob her of her small inheritance. In the amusingly exaggerated moral conclusion to the play, Quicksilver sings hymns of repentance in jail, pens a maudlin Farewell to the World (in the fashion of Robert Greene),[12] and Gertrude is forced to beg sustenance from the sister who had humbly eaten the cold scraps from "her ladyship's" sumptuous wedding feast.

The action of the main plot is focused in the opening and con-

cluding acts in which the severe moral tone, satiric characterization, and vigorous dialogue reflect the shaping hands of Marston
and Jonson rather than the touch of the more good-natured
Chapman. The middle acts shift the focus to a subplot involving
the extra-marital and extra-legal activities of Sir Petronel and
also introducing several new comic figures. Maintained throughout the central portion of the play are the tone of genial humor
and the keen sense of comic situation which reveal Chapman's
characteristic mode. Swinburne noted the stylistic resemblance
between this middle section and the other works of Chapman;
and subsequent scholars, although sometimes differing in opinion
about specific scenes, have concurred in attributing the action of
the subplot to Chapman. Although structurally constituting merely
the underplot, as Swinburne remarked, "these scenes have in them
enough of wit and humorous invention to furnish forth the whole
five acts of an ordinary comedy of intrigue." [13]

It is in the last scene of the second act that the audience learns
of Sir Petronel's duplicity, when he admits to his fellow scapegrace Quicksilver that "all the castles I have are built with air"
(II, iii, 9–10). It is also revealed that Quicksilver's mistress Sindefy
is to become Gertrude's gentlewoman and that the old usurer
Security is to lend the defunct knight some cash or commodity.
The third act opens in Security's house, where he and his new
young wife Winifred entertain Petronel, Quicksilver, and the
lawyer Bramble at a festive breakfast. Sir Petronel is engaged
in a last-minute, shady deal before embarking on a get-away
voyage to Virginia: he slyly acquires his wife's signature on a
deed of sale for her inherited property to turn over to the usurer
as security for the loan he needs. Then, while the embezzled
Lady Flash is naïvely dashing eastward by coach in search of the
non-existent castle, Sir Flash invites friends to the Blue Anchor
Tavern to drink to his own projected voyage eastward.

But Sir Petronel has more deviltry afoot before taking ship.
With a lustful eye on Security's own bride, Winnie, the deceitful
knight, gulls the old usurer into becoming his accomplice in arranging an assignation by convincing him that he desires Lawyer
Bramble's wife. Falling headlong into the trap, Security enthusi-
astically undertakes the role of procurer of his own wife, even
suggesting that the very disguise for the masked wench will be
Winifred's best gown!

The third scene of the third act provides an excellent sample of Chapman's comic forte. With his usual flair for exploiting and expanding a mere hint of a comic situation, he has produced a rollicking tavern scene, wherein Petronel and his followers drink to their journey and Security unwittingly proposes a toast to his own cuckoldry. To top it all off, the drunken embarkation ends in shipwreck in the Thames River—at the spot known as Cuckolds Haven!

Early in the scene the sailors Seagull, Spendall, and Scapethrift muse about the legendary wealth of Virginia. In a passage borrowed from Thomas More's *Utopia*,[14] Seagull explains the indifference of the new world to the gold which is so abundant there: "Why, man, all their dripping-pans and their chamber-pots are pure gold; and all the chains with which they chain up their streets are massy gold; all the prisoners they take are fettered in gold; and for rubies and diamonds, they go forth on holidays and gather 'em by the sea-shore to hang on their children's coats and stick in their caps, as commonly as our children wear saffron-gilt brooches and groats with holes in 'em" (III, iii, 27–35). Seemingly interpolated into this dialogue about the wonders of the new world is the insulting remark about the Scots that King James found so offensive and that landed the authors in prison.[15] Chapman disclaimed these "two clauses," which do in fact seem to interrupt the flow of his passage and which may well have been inserted by Marston:

"But as for them, [the Scots] there are no greater friends to Englishmen and England, when they are out on't, in the world then they are. And for my own part, I would a hundred thousand of 'em were there, for we are all one countrymen now, ye know, and we should find ten times more comfort of them there than we do here" (III, iii, 42–47).

Security and Bramble arrive to join in the merriment with Sir Petronel, his followers, and the mysteriously disguised lady. Security, deluded into relishing the prospect that his old friend is about to become cuckolded, proposes a toast to all cuckolds: "here's to all that are going eastward to-night towards Cuckold's Haven" (III, iii, 114–15). The unwitting self-mockery of the toast briefly unsettles the conscience of runaway Winnie, who begins to weep with regret; but she is promptly cheered up by none other than old Security himself, who slyly assures her that the "offence is too common to be respected" (III, iii, 135). Meanwhile, the infectious gaiety of the revelers leads to drinking of more and more carouses, and at the end of the scene a drunken crew indeed embarks despite ominous storm warnings that have just been announced.

A brief scene follows outside Security's house, where the jealous old dotard discovers his wife's absence and calls out in parody of *Richard III*, "A boat, a boat, a boat! A full hundred marks for a boat!" (III, iv, 5). The opening scene of the fourth act offers still another Chapmanesque *coup de théâtre*. To achieve exposition of the mock shipwreck in the Thames, the character of Slitgut, a butcher's apprentice, is introduced in the act of decorating a pole at the landmark of Cuckolds Haven with a pair of ox-horns. Sent by his master to install "in honour of St. Luke" these necessary ensigns of his homage at the Haven, a point below London on the south shore of the Thames, Slitgut climbs up the pole, a vantage point for seeing up and down the river. There he observes the furious storm raging and, much to his surprise, witnesses in turn first a gentlewoman, borne up by her clothes, being washed toward the shore; then an elderly man, bareheaded and glum, contemplating the gallows. Finally, he sees the two shipwrecked knights, convinced that they are on the coast of France, inquiring their whereabouts of a passerby—in French! After the pageant of shipwrecked souls, Slitgut descends the pole with an appropriate encomium to the horn:

Now will I descend my honourable prospect, the farthest seeing seamark of the world; no marvel, then, if I could see two miles about me. I hope the red tempest's anger be now over-blown, which sure, I think, Heaven sent as a punishment for profaning holy Saint Luke's memory with so ridiculous a custom. Thou dishonest satire, farewell to honest married men; farewell to all sorts and degrees of thee! Farewell, thou horn of hunger, that call'st th' Inns o'Court to their manger! Farewell, thou horn of abundance, that adornest the headsmen of the commonwealth! Farewell, thou horn of direction, that is the city lanthorn! Farewell, thou horn of pleasure, the ensign of the huntsman! Farewell, thou horn of destiny, th'ensign of the married man! Farewell, thou horn tree, that bearest nothing but stonefruit! (IV, i, 288–302)

What Professor Parrott called "the laughing spirit of true comedy" [16] is largely Chapman's contribution to this fine play of Jacobean London.

Parody of plays both current and a decade or so older lends topical interest to the play. In the opening act Quicksilver spouts scraps of several old plays, which obviously must have been still fresh in the memory of the audience, perhaps through recent revival. He tries to persuade Golding to turn gallant—citing the words of Ancient Pistol (2 *Henry IV*): "Turn good fellow, turn swaggering gallant, and let the welkin roar, and Erebus also" (I, i, 104–5). A few lines later, Quicksilver quotes that unquenchable old favorite, Thomas Kyd's *The Spanish Tragedy*—"*Who calls Jeronomo? Speak, here I am.*" (I, ii, 122). Still later, this time in impudent conversation with Touchstone, he drunkenly parodies Marlowe—"Holla, ye pampered jades of Asia!" (II, i, 87)—as well as more of *The Spanish Tragedy*. Even *Hamlet* comes in for its bit of incidental satire—as the tankard-bearer Potkin asks the footman so named, " 'Sfoot, Hamlet, are you mad?" (III, ii, 6). And Gertrude sings a variation on one of Ophelia's songs: "His head as white as milk, all flaxen was his hair; / But now he is dead, and laid in his bed, / And never will come again" (III, ii, 77–79).

A mixture of homely realism in the vein of *Shoemaker's Holiday*, of topical satire both innocent (parody of plays) and politically dangerous (slander of the Scots), of moral homily and rollicking good fun, *Eastward Ho* is a tribute to the combined talents of its three authors and is also one of the most delightful specimens of Jacobean comedy. Although Chapman's portion of the play can not be precisely ascertained, most scholars agree with Professor Parrott's conclusion that he wrote substantially all of the subplot, beginning with the last scene of act two and ending with the first scene of act four.

IV The Widow's Tears

The Widow's Tears, Chapman's last comedy, was written about 1605; and it was published in 1612 after a record of several performances at both the Blackfriars and Whitefriars theaters. A successful play, it is also the only comedy of Chapman's for which a dedication exists. Unlike its genial and buoyant predecessors, it is a satiric, even cynical play, of "more matter than mirth." [17] A mood of tragedy underlies this bitter but powerful "comedy" after which Chapman turned exclusively to the writing of tragedies. It is in effect a transitional piece between the comic and tragic phases of its author's dramatic career.

The source of the central episode in *The Widow's Tears* is Petronius' tale of the newly widowed Ephesian matron who surrendered her chastity in her husband's tomb. As it appears in the *Satyricon*,[18] the account is not so much laughable as ironic and mocking. Chapman's extensive amplifications serve both to intensify the irony and to interpolate laughter. He has enriched the germinal anecdote through the imposition of a parallel situation and deepened its implications through a caustic dialogue rich in satire and skepticism. The result is a highly effective play, with the exception of a hasty, inept fifth act.

The double plot is not structured in the usual parallel lines of action; instead, the Petronian plot grows out of the events in an analogous widow story presented initially in the play. As in *All Fools,* the heroes of the two actions are brothers, with the younger brother acting as the manipulator of both. The latter figure—Tharsalio—is not only the most vigorous and dynamic of all Chapman's comic heroes; he is also one of the best characterizations in all of his dramatic works. He is an older, hard-bitten counterpart of Rinaldo: a Rinaldo touched with the "audacity" and the worldliness of Momford.

Tharsalio introduces himself in a soliloquy with a looking-glass, a fitting symbol of his overwhelming egotism. He addresses Fortune—Rinaldo's "commandress of the world"—contemptuously, rejecting her in favor of his new goddess, Confidence, "patroness of all good spirits." He is ambitious to compensate for the fortune that he lost at birth to his older brother Lysander who "stepped into the world before me and gulled me of the land that my spirits and parts were indeed born to" (I, i, 46–48). His audacious plan is to woo the widowed Countess Eudora, who is not only superior to him socially but who has vowed enduring chastity in loyalty to the memory of her late husband.

In his assault on "that fort of chastity" he relies on speed coupled with the cynical conviction that women's vows are meaningless. He denies the charge of cynicism altogether, labeling it —as cynics usually do—"realism": "it hath refined my senses, and made me see with clear eyes, and to judge of objects as they truly are, not as they seem, and through their mask to discern the true face of things. It tells me how short-lived widows' tears are, that their weeping is in truth but laughing under a mask, that they mourn in their gowns and laugh in their sleeves" (I, i, 140–146). As he relishes the prospect of social climbing, an element of scorn for the proud, aristocratic lady whets his appetite for seduction: "that she, whose board / I might not sit at, I may board abed, / And under bring, who bore so high her head" (I, i, 180–82).

Although Tharsalio's first daring interview with Eudora is a failure, he immediately plans a second, with the aid of Arsace, the bawd. In a scene that is shockingly frank, even for the Jacobean stage, Arsace stirs the sensuality slumbering within the haughty Countess by pretending to warn her against this insatiable young man who "nine in a night made mad with his love" (II, ii, 93–94). The crude device is a success—as Arsace reports, "it took like sulphur" (II, iii, 17). In Tharsalio's second confrontation with Eudora, the imperturbable suitor is again repulsed; but not until his bold persistence has elicited from her an expression of admiration. Much to the surprise of Lysander, Tharsalio soon afterwards returns home in a splendid suit, boasting his proposed spousal rites. He glows with the spirit of his chosen deity Confidence as he gloats, "I was magnified" (III, i, 78).

Tharsalio's bold mission is crowned with achievement in the third act, in which a brief masque ritualizes his union with the Countess and her fortune. Meanwhile, however, the restless mind of the bridegroom has spawned a second daring plan. This conspiracy is sparked by his vengeful resentment of Lysander's scoffing remarks to him after the initial rebuff from the Countess and confirmed by his scorn for women's vows. Iago-like, Tharsalio incites his older brother to raging jealousy in spite of the renowned chastity of his wife Cynthia. The suspicious husband decides to pretend that he is killed in order to find out how long his widow will remain loyal to his memory. After ostensibly departing on a journey, he sends home the grim news that he has been slain by robbers. Cynthia mourns like the paragon of virtue and fidelity that her name and reputation proclaim. Her son Lycus eloquently describes her expression of grief to Tharsalio, who dismisses his lyrical account with the curt remark: "in prose, thou wept'st" (IV, i, 49). Meanwhile, the widow has retired with her servant Ero to her husband's tomb where the two keep vigil without sustenance for five days. Lysander now assumes the garb of a soldier whose duty is to stand guard over the crucified bodies of criminals in the cemetery to prevent their being stolen from the gibbets and surreptitiously buried. So disguised, he enters the tomb to persuade the women to leave their subterranean prison. Ero yields first, not so much in response to his persuasive words as to his even more seductive bottle of wine; and he leaves, only to return in the evening. By then Cynthia, restored from her fast by a draught of wine, is ready to toast the visitor.

In the opening scene of the fifth act, Tharsalio, who has just conceded that his faithful sister-in-law is an exception to his generalization about women, comes by the tomb only to discover, to his gleeful surprise, the figures of Cynthia and a soldier locked in embrace. Vindicated in his cynicism, he breaks into dance and song, ironically singing John Dowland's popular lyrical tribute to "She, she, she, and none but she! / She only queen of love and chastity" (V, i, 31–32). Unquestionably a theatrical coup, the scene is one more illustration of Chapman's keen sense of comic situation. Tharsalio now jauntily schemes to get the soldier into trouble by stealing one of the crucified bodies.

Up to this point Chapman has followed Petronius, except for making the soldier the husband in disguise, a facet of the legend which actually belongs to an even earlier source. Furthermore, he has heightened it dramatically and thematically through the analogous widow plot. But a drastic change suddenly occurs in the characterization of Cynthia, and from that point on, the play as a whole degenerates rapidly. The newly enamored widow has brutally suggested—as in Petronius—the substitution of her husband's corpse for the missing crucified body. Shocked at her callousness, Lysander unexpectedly declares that it was he who murdered the husband. Cynthia hesitates scarcely enough to be even polite: "Would I had never seen thee, or heard sooner / This bloody story; yet see, note my truth, / Yet I must love thee" (V, ii, 34–36). And as she goes on to berate the soldier for his squeamishness, she becomes a monster, a caricature rather than a character. She huskily volunteers to help drag the corpse to the cross, until Lysander, almost sickened with disgust, leaves for a crowbar—and a breath of air.

After this virtual collapse of the Lysander-Cynthia plot, a desperate final scene dissolves rather than resolves the action. The scene is the graveyard, and the opening banter of the soldiers echoes the overall cynicism of the play: "in this topsy-turvy world friendship and bosom-kindness are but made covers for mischief, means to compass ill. Near-allied trust is but a bridge for treason. The presumptions cry loud against him, his answers sound disjointed, cross-legged, tripping up one another" (V, iii, 33–37).

And, in complete perversion of justice, the Governor,[19] who is called in to restore order, is "a most brainless, imperious upstart": "O desert, where wast thou when this wooden dagger was gilded over with the title of Governor?" (V, iii, 221–23). The wooden dagger identifies him with the traditional Vice, and Tharsalio remarks of him that "the Vice must snap his authority at all he meets; how shall't else be known what part he plays?" (V, iii, 275–76). But even more than this morality figure, he resembles the traditional Lord of Misrule whose function is to invert hierarchy and disrupt order. He vows "I'll turn all topsy-turvy" (V, iii, 285), and his plans are so calculated: "Fools shall have wealth, and the learned shall live by their wits. I'll have no more bankrouts. They that owe money shall pay it at their best leisure, and the rest shall make a virtue of imprisonment, and their wives shall help to pay their debts" (V, iii, 310–14). But Tharsalio interrupts his foolish speech by reminding him of the wedding ceremony awaiting his official presence. Admittedly at a "non plus," the Governor agrees to perform his proper role in uniting Lycus, son of Lysander, and Laodice, daughter of Eudora.

Although not the best of Chapman's comedies *qua* comedy, *The Widow's Tears* is his most powerful play this side of tragedy. Tharsalio, a superb characterization, overshadows the other male roles although the haughty and temperamental Eudora is almost equally effective on a smaller scale. Intimations of Tharsalio's character had appeared in Valerio's love of gulling others, in Rinaldo's opportunism, and in Lodovico's restless energy; but, unlike these earlier intriguers, Tharsalio is divested alike of all ideals and all illusions. He also lacks their innocent good humor, for his wit has a cutting edge. His insultingly negative view of human nature contrasts to his supremely confident opinion of his own powers. Even more than a consummation of preceding comic heroes, he is a harbinger of tragic heroes to follow. In particular, he is a precursor to that tragic second son, Bussy d'Ambois. As Bussy will do, Tharsalio rejects Fortune in favor of his own overwhelming *Virtù*.[20] Also like Bussy he seeks to dominate his world through knowledge, but in both cases it is the limited knowledge of things without benefit of the deeper knowledge of self. In the context of comedy—albeit a marginal comedy—Tharsalio succeeds whereas both of the Herculean heroes cast in his mold, Bussy and Byron, must fail.

CHAPTER 5

Herculean Heroes

LIKE Chapman's career as a writer of comedies his work as a tragedian divides into two distinct phases. This division does not indicate a shift in dramaturgy but one in the nature of the tragic heroes, all of whom completely dominate their dramatic milieu. In the first three tragedies—*Bussy D'Ambois, Byron's Conspiracy,* and *Byron's Tragedy*—the heroes are Herculean figures: men of action and arrogant individualists, but inevitable victims of their own over-weening ambitions. The language of these plays abounds in allusions to the myth of Hercules and in actual paraphrase of Seneca's dramatization, *Hercules Furens.* In the last three tragedies—*Revenge of Bussy, Chabot, Caesar and Pompey*—the Herculean adventurer is supplanted by a philosophical figure, the "Senecal man," whose fortitude and patience obviate anger and aggression and whose victories are inward, achieved in the camps of mind and spirit rather than on the fields of bodily encounter. As Ennis Rees has pointed out in his study of Chapman's tragedies,[1] the early dramatic heroes correspond to the Achillean ideal exalted in the *Iliad,* but the later exemplify the Odyssean prototype of wisdom over warfare, the ideal of Chapman's more mature translation.

The Herculean plays are also more typically Jacobean in their language, theme, and technique than are their reflective, relatively static successors. Although Bussy and Byron are worthy descendants of the Marlovian hyperbolic hero, they are cast into the peculiarly Jacobean atmosphere, with its persistent lament for disorder, its intensity of gloom and disillusionment, its flavor of corruption, and its primitivistic nostalgia for an earlier golden day when nature was good and when men were natural. And the tragic vehicles in which the characters move to the purifying flame which proves to be a sacrificial pyre, are filled with the sensational episodes and spectral visitations which so delighted the turn-of-the-century audience.

All of the tragedies, however, are united by a common central theme and by a focus on the same basic conflicts: their philosophical content should be interpreted in terms of a progression rather than of an opposition. Their unifying theme is knowledge, which underlies all of Chapman's verse but is treated in these plays more seriously and speculatively than elsewhere. The tragic heroes, unlike their comic predecessors, learn to disdain mere objective knowledge of the world and its application in intrigue; with their intimation of a higher, more spiritual knowledge, they engage in conflicts between passion and reason, fortune and virtue, fate and freedom. Their own progression through tragic events leads them from an objective knowledge of the world to a subjective one of the self.

In the Renaissance world view, a web of analogies united the microcosm man with the macrocosm in which he lived. One such correspondence was recognized between the major levels of creation and of knowledge. The stages of creation were believed to represent a path moving upward from mere "being" to "self-consciousness." "Being," the lowest level, was common to everything that exists, and the world of nature encompassed the intermediary levels of "living" and "feeling"; but only man embodied the highest level, "reason," which in turn attained its highest goal in reflexive knowledge. Creation thus moved through several stages in order to arrive finally at its own self-conception. Similarly, the knowledge of man moved upward from the world to himself. For man to know only the phenomenal world below him was not true wisdom. Insofar as his knowledge was only objective, he was, in fact, only potentially man—*homo in potentia.* The fully realized man—*homo in actu*—was the fully self-conscious man.

The truly wise man who had ascended to the lofty level of genuine self-knowledge had thereby reconciled the traditional tensions within the microcosm between fate and free will, fortune and virtue, passion and reason. The merely potential man who had not reached that highest stage of knowledge was ruled by fate and joined the lists of fortune. He was not free, for freedom had to be acquired through inner wisdom. Such a man, regardless of his abilities, was victimized by events: manly virtù did not suffice to overcome vicissitude unless fulfilled by its inward counterpart, virtue. And such a man was ruled by his passions, the violent forces of nature residing within. Only reason, applied to the acquisition of self-knowledge, could overrule the dictates of nature. Chapman's Bussy and Byron are such potential men. Rich in natural endowments and in worldly attributes, strong in their external virtù, they are nonetheless slaves to their own passions and subject to fate. Their ultimate redemption as tragic heroes, however, is symbolized by the fiery imagery of their final moments, for fire, the highest of the four elements, signifies the highest level of knowledge.[2]

I Bussy D'Ambois

Bussy D'Ambois, Chapman's first experiment in tragedy, has remained his most popular play. Composed for the Children of the Chapel, it was subsequently performed by the rival children's company at St. Paul's, later revised for a fresh production at Whitefriars, and eventually performed by the King's men. This hardy drama even returned to the post-Restoration theater; and, although it was scathingly denounced by the neo-Classic critic Dryden,[3] it was an enormous success on the stage of his time. *Bussy D'Ambois* possesses the vigor of language, strength of characterization, and theatricality of episode that represent Jacobean tragedy at its height of power, as well as some of those excesses in bombast and sensationalism that led to its decline.

Although the exact source of this tragic drama is not known, it is based on the actual career of a Renaissance soldier-courtier-adventurer: Louis de Clermont d'Amboise, Seigneur de Bussy, who was born in 1549. The original figure was a daring soldier, often wounded in battle, and a hot-tempered courtier in constant conflict with the minions of the king. While acting as governor of Anjou, an honor conferred on him by Monsieur, the next younger brother of King Henry III, he met and successfully wooed the wife of Montsoreau, Grand Huntsman to Monsieur. The king's brother then betrayed his protégé by revealing an incriminating letter to King Henry, who in turn showed it to the irate husband, who forced his wife at pistol point to invite Bussy to their castle; there he was ambushed and murdered on his arrival. The young victim of this adulterous intrigue was mourned at Court despite his insolent career there, and praised for excellence by everyone, including his former enemies.

Chapman's tragic dramatization of Bussy's meteoric career enriched the historical account in several ways. The playwright exploited the stock Senecan techniques of sensationalism so popular at that time. Not one but several ghosts appear in response to incantation; and, less spectral but more shocking, the enraged Montsurry stabs his wife repeatedly—in full view of the audience —and then subjects her wounded body to the torture of the rack. Chapman also intensified the language of his play with a thickly textured rhetoric in the Senecan vein. A nocturnal atmosphere pervades the play—like the "murky" hell of *Macbeth*—and the imagery sparkles with candles and meteors that flame in the darkness. A ghost that appears as a gleam in the dark is startling with its "sudden flash." Tamyra's fine evocation of the "peaceful regents of the night" is but one of many rhetorical glorifications of night. Bussy is introduced by Monsieur as "A man of spirit beyond the reach of fear, / Who (discontent with his neglected worth) / Neglects the light, and loves obscure abodes" (I, i, 46–48); and Monsieur advises him accordingly: "Do thou but bring / Light to the banquet Fortune sets before thee, / And thou wilt loathe lean darkness like thy death" (I, i, 61–3). This heroic figure whose "words and looks / Are like the flashes and the bolts of Jove" (I, i, 36–7) is eulogized by the Umbra (the ghost of the Friar) at the end of the play:

> Farewell, brave relics of a complete man,
> Look up and see thy spirit made a star;
> Join flames with Hercules, and when thou sett'st
> Thy radiant forehead in the firmament,
> Make the vast crystal crack with thy receipt;
> Spread to a world of fire, and the aged sky
> Cheer with new sparks of old humanity. (V, iv, 147–53)

The dialogue throughout the play dazzles with its brilliant, concrete imagery.

But even more important, Chapman heightened the bold but obvious plot with a complex, interior characterization of his hero and with provocative philosophical speculation. At first Bussy is clearly a descendant of Rinaldo and Tharsalio. Like his comic prototypes, he is an impoverished second son, a victim of wanton Fortune, whose blindness he condemns even as he acknowledges its power: "Fortune, not Reason, rules the state of things, / Reward goes backwards, Honour on his head" (I, i, 1–2). But he is also much more, for the dialogue which unfolds his tragic history wrestles with ultimate questions about the nature and destiny of man. He echoes the complaint of Hamlet that the world is out of joint; and, like Webster's malcontent Bosola, he rails at a society in which worth is unrewarded but fraud flourishes. His long opening soliloquy is an eloquent version of the Jacobean lament, "all coherence gone," [4] including the existential remark: "Man is a torch borne in the wind; a dream / But of a shadow, summ'd with all his substance" (I, i, 19–20).

Although Bussy dominates the play as Marlowe's Titan heroes did, there lurks in his overpowering role an ambiguity and complexity from which the clear, luminous Marlovian figures were free. One is never in doubt as to Tamburlaine's intentions; one is never quite sure of Bussy's. Certainly it is oversimplification to label Chapman's first tragic hero with a single epithet, whether that of Renaissance individualist or that of stoic hero, as some critics have done; [5] for he is both of these and more. Bussy's individualism is shot through with the tension and paradox of Jacobean pessimism, and his stoicism is tempered by rebellion and defiance. Further complicating his role is the apparent lack of what Eliot called an "objective correlative" [6] for the praises heaped upon him throughout the play. Indeed, the first noble deed of this duelling, arrogant adulterer occurs at the very end of the play, when, in response to his paramour's plea, he spares the life of her husband, whom he has just defeated in hand-to-hand combat. But even here the ironic Fates scorn the gesture as if mocking its intention: random shots from out of sight strike and kill Bussy in his first moment of generosity.

Some of the apparent contradictions in the play are reconciled, however, by taking sufficiently into account the evolving nature of Bussy's role during the course of the tragic action; not a static figure, he acquires his tragic stature only gradually. The Bussy of the opening scene is scarcely an impressive figure, although the Machiavellian Monsieur praises him as "A man of spirit beyond the reach of fear" (I, i, 46). The initial dialogue between them focuses on the timely theme of corruption at court, with its rampant flattery, hypocrisy, and self-seeking aggrandizement. But Monsieur politically hints that the wheel of Fortune may soon be in the ascendancy for the impoverished soldier-poet Bussy; and he leaves with a promise to send a gift. Alone again, Bussy wryly speculates that he may introduce a new fashion at court—Honesty.

When Monsieur's steward, Maffe, returns with a gift of a thousand crowns, he hides it, reluctant to turn it over to the ragged soldier. His rude insolence is challenged by Bussy, who first shames him into conceding the entire amount, then strikes him—"for your aptness to dispute" (I, i, 221). Bussy's entry into court circles is scarcely less vehement, confirming Maffe's prediction that the crowns will spill blood again. "A courtier rotten before he is ripe," Bussy boldly sues for the favors of the Duchess of Guise; and he rashly arouses the ire of the Duke of Guise and his followers, with the grim result that he takes on three of the latter in a duel. The bloody action of the duel is reported in epic language by a messenger, as is the result: only Bussy survives. Monsieur then pleads the case of his brash protégé before King Henry, who consents to spare his life. Hardly grateful for the royal mercy, Bussy asserts his individualistic credo in a manner hardly complimentary to his ruler: "Who to himself is law, no law doth need, / Offends no law, and is a king indeed" (II, i, 203–4). These words recall a similar remark made by Strozza; but, whereas the stoic Strozza exemplified the principle in action, Bussy merely asserts it in theory. The passionate French courtier does not know himself well enough to be his own law.

But he readily learns the courtly art of hypocrisy, admitting that his overt play for the Duchess is but a façade for his intrigue with Tamyra, Countess of Montsurry, who is also the current object of Monsieur's attentions. Tamyra is also no stranger to hypocrisy, for her virtuous indignation over the advances of Monsieur is followed promptly by arrangements for an assignation with Bussy. But the supreme example of hypocrisy, reflecting the utter corruption of court morality, is the friar who acts as a go-between for the lovers and who leads Bussy to his chosen mistress through a secret passage under cover of night—while he offers him worldly advice about the art of handling women.

After their assignation Bussy taunts Tamyra's "nice" conscience

which "bites too hotly of the Puritan spice" (III, i, 2). He scorns
Sin as a mere sham; it is painted to look monstrous by Policy.
Whereas Bussy dismisses Sin in favor of a decorous secrecy,
Tamyra rationalizes her guilt as that "finger of nature" which
weakens all women. Enslaved to her passions, she is the victim
of fate; and her surrender to her lower nature is both quick and
total. She does not grow in knowledge; and, even after the tragic
consequences of her amorous adventure, she regrets only that she
did not keep a better secret.

Throughout the court scenes in the middle acts of the play,
Bussy plays the role of satirical malcontent. In one such scene,
occurring after his adulterous conquest, he attacks the rampant
sensuality and greed of clergyman, lawyers, and courtiers—and
he does so in the traditional moral manner of didactic literature.
His language is rife with images of decadence and bestiality.
Bussy's own character, however, is contrasted to the pervasive
decadence of contemporary society. In a spirited defense of his
frank new courtier, King Henry praises Bussy's "natural" virtue,
which harks back to the golden age before men became degenerate:

> Kings had never borne
> Such boundless empire over other men,
> Had all maintain'd the spirit and state of D'Ambois;
> Nor had the full impartial hand of Nature
> That all things gave in her original,
> Without these definite terms of Mine and Thine,
> Been turn'd unjustly to the hand of Fortune,
> Had all preserv'd her in her prime, like D'Ambois;
> No envy, no disjunction had dissolv'd,
> Or pluck'd one stick out of the golden faggot
> In which the world of Saturn bound our lives,
> Had all been held together with the nerves,
> The genius, and th'ingenuous soul of D'Ambois. (III, ii, 95–107)

But Monsieur coolly refutes this romantic justification. He attributes Bussy's admitted heroism to mere impulsive violence and,
while granting him "strange gifts in nature," adds that "no soul"
diffuses them to make him a whole man. Monsieur's position is in
keeping with the Renaissance interpretation of reason as the
power in man by which nature completes her cycle of develop-

ment. Once man abandons the simplicity of his original state of "natural" virtue, he must go through the levels of knowledge until he arrives at self-knowledge in order to rediscover his relationship with nature. Otherwise, he remains permanently retarded, so to speak, on the sub-humanistic level of attainment. With his "natural" virtues exploded, Bussy retorts with a vitriolic account of Monsieur's policy. A man who "did never good but to do ill" (III, ii, 467), and "a hypocrite who jests with God while he bargains with the devil," Monsieur is indeed a Machiavellian; but he does possess a knowledge of the world which momentarily places him above the heroic but innocent, the "great" but not "good" Bussy.[7]

Even the bitter social satire voiced by Bussy in the play is overshadowed, however, by the cosmic complaints registered by several other characters in speeches of choral commentary. One such passage occurs in the bloody melodrama of the fifth act, in which Montsurry, maddened by jealousy and shame, tortures Tamyra in order to force her to summon Bussy by drafting a letter in her own blood. The cuckolded husband does not experience his ultimate disillusionment until the friar enters, with drawn sword, only to drop dead on the spot from heart failure. Only at this moment does Montsurry realize the ironic fact that this holy man has acted as go-between in the adultery. He suddenly perceives the universal scheme of things gone awry:

> The too huge bias of the world hath sway'd
> Her back-part upwards, and with that she braves
> This hemisphere, that long her mouth hath mock'd!
> The gravity of her religious face,
> (Now grown too weighty with her sacrilege,
> And here discern'd sophisticate enough)
> Turns to th'Antipodes; and all the forms
> That her illusions have impress'd in her,
> Have eaten through her back; and now all see,
> How she is riveted with hypocrisy. (V, i, 163–73)

After this crucial scene, Monsieur and Guise appear together on stage to deliver set speeches, quite out of character, in a digressive philosophical colloquy. Monsieur offers a futile and deterministic view of life in which all things are at the mercy of of a blind, wanton, and utterly purposeless Nature:

> Now shall we see that Nature hath no end
> In her great works responsive to their worths;
> That she, that makes so many eyes and souls
> To see and foresee, is stark blind herself;
> And as illiterate men say Latin prayers
> By rote of heart and daily iteration,
> Not knowing what they say, so Nature lays
> A deal of stuff together, and by use,
> Or by the mere necessity of matter,
> Ends such a work, fills it, or leaves it empty
> Of strength or virtue, error or clear truth,
> Not knowing what she does. (V, ii, 1–12)

Although this pessimistic view is voiced by the Machiavellian villain, the speech is too divorced from the demands of characterization to be dismissed as such. The words assert a materialistic skepticism deeply embedded in the context of the play and reaching well beyond the range of one character's doubts. The limitation of the view suits the speaker, however, for he remains low in the hierarchy of knowledge. Mere nature is in itself blind; but, when nature fulfills her upward evolution in the form of human reason, she can complete her cycle and know herself. It is precisely such a man as Bussy, strong in valor and virtue but deficient in self-knowledge, who is destined to be the supreme victim of a wanton nature. Lacking himself the human wisdom needed to invest nature with meaning, he must yield to her consequent meaninglessness. The "mere necessity of matter" confines the spokesman, Monsieur, and the victim, Bussy; but it by no means inhibits the range of transcendent human reason.

Bussy achieves an intimation of such transcendent possibility in the last act of the play, in which he rises to a stoic stature that retroactively justifies the extravagant praises received earlier. Finally aware that he is mortally wounded when the aimless shots strike him down, he laments the frailty of a spirit that must yield to the exigency of a wounded body:

> Is my body, then,
> But penetrable flesh? And must my mind
> Follow my blood? Can my divine part add
> No aid to th'earthly in extremity?
> Then these divines are but for form, not fact:

> Man is of two sweet courtly friends compact,
> A mistress and a servant: let my death
> Define life nothing but a courtier's breath.
> Nothing is made of nought, of all things made,
> Their abstract being a dream but of a shade. (V, iv, 78–87)

As his knowledge at last reaches upward, he vows to "look up-
wards even in death." Professing to bear "an equal thought" of
life and death, he insists upon dying while standing. His final
words express his tragic waste of natural gifts not refined by
Learning:

> O frail condition of strength, valour, virtue
> In me (like warning fire upon the top
> Of some steep beacon, on a steeper hill)
> Made to express it: like a falling star
> Silently glanc'd, that like a thunderbolt
> Look'd to have stuck and shook the firmament. (V, iv, 141–46)

Natural gifts are not enough. Simple Herculean heroism was
consumed by flames even in the golden age, and in the modern
world its spark signals a falling star, not a thunderbolt. To
transcend, or even to challenge, one's fortune requires the acquired gifts of learning, discipline, and wisdom—the gifts to be
admirably demonstrated by Bussy's brother Clermont.

Bussy is not unsympathetically presented—his fate evokes
genuine tragic pity—but it would be a mistake to assume Chapman's sympathy with his untutored individualism. The brash ex-
ploits of the courtier are impressive but not reasonable. His virtù
lacks the dimension of self-control. Wisdom must function within
the man as king over his passions before he liberates himself
from bondage to external kingship. Authority must and will function, either without as law or within as discipline. Bussy is praised
for his heroic instincts and his Herculean potentiality which, like
untempered steel, are strong but brittle. Bussy will join flames
with Hercules, and his forehead will make the vast firmament
crack with the force of his ascent; but only scholarly Clermont,
master of himself, can, or will, cope with the Machiavellian policy
of the modern court.

II The Conspiracy of Charles, Duke of Byron

The approximate date of the double play *The Conspiracy and Tragedy of Charles, Duke of Byron* is easily ascertained because of the censorship difficulties it encountered. In his dedication to Walsingham, Chapman lamented the state of these "poor dismembered poems," for the fourth act of the *Conspiracy* was completely cut away and a second-hand report of Byron's ambassage to England was substituted for the enactment of the actual visit. What were probably the most dramatic scenes of the *Tragedy*, involving the confrontation of Henry IV's queen and his mistress, have also disappeared. At least one reason for the drastic censorship was stated in an indignant letter of the French ambassador, La Boderie, translated as follows:

April 8, 1608, I caused certain players to be forbid from acting the history of the Duke of Byron; when, however, they saw that the whole Court had left the town, they persisted in acting it; nay, they brought upon the stage the Queen of France and Mademoiselle de Verneuil. The former, having accosted the latter with very hard words, gave her a box on the ear. At my suit three of them [i.e., the players] were arrested, but the principal person, the author, escaped.[8]

The evident date of the double tragedy is therefore late 1607 or early 1608.

The source of the plays is again French history: this time Chapman turned to Grimeston's *General Inventorie of the History of France*. The original Charles de Gontant, Baron de Biron, was well known to Englishmen who had heard of his ambassage to Queen Elizabeth, her dire warning to him based on the recent fate of the traitorous Essex, and his subsequent death by execution in fulfillment of that analogy. Biron had been a renowned soldier and a favorite of Henry IV, who had rewarded him profusely for his military victories by both gifts and honors. Ever restless and dissatisfied, however, the ambitious young warrior had engaged in intrigue against his king and benefactor until Henry, hearing of these misguided adventures, wisely reprimanded and generously forgave the headstrong young man. But the ambitious Biron became wayward in his loyalties, and this time the King had no choice but to make an example of him for his treason. Biron refused to believe in the reality of his death sentence until the very end, and the account of his last rebellious hours and faltering execution is filled with both horror and pathos. Since Chapman followed his source closely, several of Biron's speeches are merely transformed into blank verse. Without actually modifying the historical content, however, the playwright introduced structural changes into the sequence of events to achieve effective dramaturgic contrast.

The Byron plays (using the anglicized form of the hero's name) have often been called dramatic poems, a label in part justified by Chapman's own reference to them as "poems" in his dedication. As a criticism of their inherent dramatic quality, however, the term is not accurate. Although they have none of the ostentatiously theatrical Senecan machinery which distinguished *Bussy D'Ambois*, they have the conflict which is the essence of drama. This conflict is not primarily physical: there are no duels, no torture scenes, not even a single ghost to spur the action. But both psychological and thematic conflicts are sustained throughout the plays. Byron is a fully realized character by virtue of his internal conflict, and the thematic conflict between individualism and enlightened authority is presented and resolved in a series of brilliant debates in dialogue.

Chapman's prologue offers a didactic commentary on the career of his hero that recalls the epilogue to Marlowe's *Dr. Faustus*. Whatever emotional sympathies Chapman may have felt for the brave warrior and aspiring individualist, his moral condemnation of Byron's treachery and its precipitating pride is explicit enough. The final couplet, which summarizes the tragic implications of Byron's life, would serve for Bussy as well: "And see in his revolt how honour's flood / Ebbs into air, when men are great, not good" (11. 23–24). The *Conspiracy* opens with a scene of Machiavellian policy in action. The Duke of Savoy is seeking "discontented spirits" at the Court of France to aid his destructive designs against that kingdom. Roncas, his Parisian ambassador, suggests two likely candidates: the Machiavellian villain of the piece, La Fin, and that "man of Matchless valour," Byron. Roncas knows Byron's fundamental weakness:

>   that humour
> Is fit to feed his spirits, whom it possesseth,
> With faith in any error, chiefly where

Men blow it up with praise of his perfections;
The taste whereof in him so soothes his palate,
And takes up all his appetite, that oft-times
He will refuse his meat and company
To feast alone with their most strong conceit. (I, i, 70–78)

When the King appears on stage, the opposition between royal nobility and court policy is clearly established in a scene that is naturalistically untenable but dramatically effective in its homiletic clarity. After banishing La Fin for his threatening spirit of dissension, Henry directs to his model of political wickedness a most undiplomatic insult: "A man must think of all the villainies / He knows in all men to decipher thee, / That art the centre to impiety" (I, i, 159–61).

The initial appearance of Byron is delayed until the second scene when dramatically appropriate circumstances are provided. For, although this play lacks overt physical action, it illustrates well Chapman's abiding flair for theatrical situation. An example of his dramatic sensibility is the episode in which the Machiavellian Picoté subtly seduces Byron to his cause by spreading a carpet embroidered with the history of Rome so that the susceptible ego of the Duke will respond to the lure of Roman conquest under his tread. As Picoté expected, Byron's ambition is immediately fired.

'Tis immortality to die aspiring,
As if a man were taken quick to heaven;
What will not hold perfection, let it burst;
        . . . happy Semele,
That died compress'd with glory! Happiness
Denies comparison of less or more,
And not at most, is nothing: like the shaft
Shot at the sun by angry Hercules,
And into shivers by the thunder broken,
Will I be if I burst; and in my heart
This shall be written: 'Yet 'twas high and right.' (I, ii, 31–33, 37–44)

Picoté pursues his seductive statecraft with that materialistic denigration of ideals conventionally associated with the notorious and cynical procedures approved by Machiavelli.[9] He dismisses the meaningful abstractions as mere words: "Your Excellency knows that simple loyalty, / Faith, love, sincerity, are but words, no things, / Merely devis'd for form" (I, ii, 116–18). Byron is easy prey for this sort of specious appeal combined with flattery. Quite aware of this weakness, King Henry decides to send him on a trip to England:

> To breathe a while in temperate English air,
> Where lips are spic'd with free and loyal counsels,
> Where policies are not ruinous, but saving;
> Wisdom is simple, valour righteous,
> Human, and hating facts of brutish forces;
> And whose grave natures scorn the scoffs of France,
> The empty compliments of Italy,
> The any-way encroaching pride of Spain,
> And love men modest, hearty, just, and plain. (II, ii, 49–56)

Meanwhile, however, Savoy is plotting with La Fin to alienate the king from Byron. His "politic" plan is to praise the Duke so excessively before the King that Henry will resent the implicit comparison as derogatory to himself. The diplomatic strategy is successful, and, rather defensively, Henry praises the noble English generals who aided him in his campaign as equal in valor to the redoubtable Byron. When Savoy reports the King's slight directly to Byron, he becomes enraged. With clever dramaturgic contrast, Chapman has the Savoyards engaged throughout the scene in extravagant praise of a portrait of Byron which is being painted. The boundless egotism of the man, inflamed by the insult, permits him to volunteer a description of the statue he will have made, which is intended to exceed the painting in majesty and to be located in Amiens, the city he so gloriously defended. When Henry appears on the scene to scold Byron for being seen in the company of "La Fiend," the Duke's sudden show of virtue is more vocal than convincing. Henry reminds his minion allegorically that Treason—"to a credulous age"—comes invisible, "veil'd with flattery."

Taken directly from Grimeston, the next scene depicts Byron's visit to a noted astrologer, La Brosse, in order to have his horoscope cast. Even before the disguised figure of Byron appears to him, La Brosse voices a foreboding that the hour presages ill for himself. Although he does not recognize the man who brings in the horoscope, he accurately interprets the owner as a man of noble parts and princely valor. Unfortunately, the future is marred by a "Caput Algol," [10] a phrase so ominous that he is reluctant even to explain its meaning. Byron urges the fearful man to speak, threatening otherwise to seek the answer by laying his brain "here scatter'd at my feet." When La Brosse hesitantly informs him that the phrase signifies that Byron will lose his head, he responds in a fury by brutally beating the poor man. Over the prostrate figure of the half-dead astrologer, he shamefully admits that he would have preferred flattery to truth: "Would I had given thee twenty thousand crowns / That thou had'st flatter'd me" (III, iii, 95–96). But Byron suddenly regains his old spirit of defiance, and with a scornful rejection of the prediction he utters the most famous lines of the play:

> be free, all worthy spirits,
> And stretch yourselves for greatness and for height,
> Untruss your slaveries; you have height enough
> Beneath this steep heaven to use all your reaches;
> 'Tis too far off to let you, or respect you.
> Give me a spirit that on this life's rough sea
> Loves t'have his sails fill'd with a lusty wind,
> Even till his sail-yards tremble, his masts crack,
> And his rapt ship run on her side so low
> That she drinks water, and her keel plows air.
> There is no danger to a man that knows
> What life and death is; there's not any law
> Exceeds his knowledge; neither is it lawful
> That he should stoop to any other law.
> He goes before them, and commands them all,
> That to himself is a law rational. (III, iii, 130–45)

The mute figure of the abused astrologer comments ironically on the bravado of the speech. The words are true, but they are not true of Byron: they contain the ideal of goodness added to greatness, but Byron is the very incarnation of mere outward greatness without that inner goodness which is knowledge. Obviously Byron is anything but a law to himself. Like Bussy, he asserts a freedom of will which is not a reality for him because he has submitted to his own base ego. In the eternal conflict between Fortune and Virtue, the hotheaded Byrons, although momentary favorites of Fortune's whim, are always in danger of a "caput

algol," for they do not know what life and death are. Byron, who,
like Bussy, has not attained the self-conscious level of knowledge,
is a slave to astrology, a plaything of the stars. Although his
knowledge of the world is superior to that of Bussy, his remarks
on Virtue betray the same externality and shallowness that characterized the naïve courtier. In spite of his aggressive ego-mania,
Byron must therefore remain subject to the authority of King
Henry precisely because he does not possess the inward authority
he says he has.

All that remains of the truncated fourth act is Crequi's lengthy
report of Byron's ambassage to England. One will probably never
know whether Chapman dared to depict Queen Elizabeth point-
ing out the moldering heads of traitors to the treasonous visitor
from France.

A dramatic confrontation of Byron and King Henry opens the
fifth act. Misled by the politic advice of Savoy and La Fin, Byron
overreaches his claim on the generosity of the king by resquesting
the honor of retaining the citadel of Bourg, which he had captured. Henry denies the boon, partly for political reasons and
partly, as he reluctantly admits, because Byron is suspected of
having had communication with his enemies. Byron's fury sput-
ters out his indignation, only to draw the laughter of the king as
his boasts become more and more hyperbolic. Byron is stunned
by the insulting mockery: "What's grave in earth, what awful,
what abhorr'd, / If my rage be ridiculous? I will make it / The
law and rule of all things serious" (V, ii, 1–3).

The dramatic conflict between sovereign and subject is brought
full circle as Henry summons Byron to return to his presence and,
with the forceful rhetoric of authority, subdues the rebellious
noble who kneels before him, repentant. It is a loyal subject who
proclaims: "If ever I did good I lock'd it safe / In you, th'impregnable defence of goodness; / If ill, I press it with my penitent
knees / To that unsounded depth whence nought returneth" (V,
ii, 103–106). In the concluding episode, Byron haughtily refuses
the gifts designated for him by the department Savoy.

The philosophical level of the conflict transposes the hierarchical relationship into the realm of learning: King Henry is
qualified for sovereignty by an inner wisdom which supports his
external office whereas the passionate Byron, who cannot control
himself, is fated never to rule others. Guided by Virtue, the wise

ruler struggles not only against Fortune's minion, Byron, but also against the corrupted courtiers who try to mislead princes with their own fallacious knowledge.

III   The Tragedy of Charles, Duke of Byron

The Tragedy resumes the action shortly after the conclusion of *The Conspiracy.* King Henry has just learned, to his astonishment and regret, that Byron's loyalty has relapsed. He sadly surveys the extensive honors awarded the hero whose overweening ambition will apparently be satisfied with nothing less than the crown. Confidently bequeathing the monarchy to his own son, Henry puts a sword into the hand of the young Dauphin and prophesies a brilliant future for him as king; but history had other plans for the boy who became Louis XIII.

In Byron's first appearance, he complains bitterly about his neglected merit. In the manner of Bussy, he interprets his own supposed mistreatment as evidence of a perverse world: "The world is quite inverted, Virtue thrown / At Vice's feet, and sensual Peace confounds / Valour and cowardice, fame and infamy" (I, ii, 14–16). But the choral theme of perversion echoed throughout the play finds its proper focus in Byron himself, who plans to destroy France for the sole purpose of gratifying his ego through building it up again: "I, who through all the dangers than can siege / The life of man have forc'd my glorious way / To the repairing of my country's ruins, / Will ruin it again to re-advance it" (I, ii, 32–35). But Byron's very egotism which dotes on the gross flattery of La Fin is self-blinding and destructive: Byron does not even suspect the duplicity of that Machiavellian courtier who reveals the whole conspiracy to the king. Since self-knowledge and knowledge of the world are in a sense similar processes moving in opposite directions, Byron fails in both the microcosmic and the macrocosmic realms. His ego is too blind to find itself by turning to the world, and his comprehension of the world is blocked by the distortions of his ego. The truths of the major *mundus* and the minor *mundus* elude him.

The conclusion of the first act and the beginning of the second were apparently cut away by the censor. The only extant scene of the second act, a Masque at Court, is based on an episode in Grimeston. The leading ladies in the masque are Henry's queen, Marie de Medici, as Chastity, and his mistress, Henriette D'En-

tragues, as Liberality. The masque, which represents a reconciliation of the two women in the monarch's life, must have satisfied the sensibilities of even the French ambassador. More central
to the theme of the play, the masque also signifies the justice and
harmony on the side of the fallible but enlightened ruler.

Byron opens the third act with an address on Machiavellian
"policy." [11] After describing that new school of statecraft founded
in Italy and threatening to undermine the authority of princes,
he disregards his own seditious designs while he proceeds to eu-
logize the divine right of kings:

> Religion is a branch, first set and blest
> By Heaven's high finger in the hearts of kings,
> Which whilom grew into a goodly tree;
> Bright angels sat and sung upon the twigs,
> And royal branches for the heads of kings
> Were twisted of them; but since squint-eyed Envy
> And pale Suspicion dash'd the heads of kingdoms
> One gainst another, two abhorred twins,
> With two foul tails, stern War and Liberty,
> Enter'd the world. The tree that grew from heaven
> Is overrun with moss; the cheerful music
> That heretofore hath sounded out of it
> Begins to cease; and as she casts her leaves,
> By small degrees the kingdoms of the earth
> Decline and wither; and look, whensoever
> That the pure sap in her is dried-up quite,
> The lamp of all authority goes out,
> And all the blaze of princes is extinct. (III, i, 25–42)

The contradiction between Byron's avowed loyalty to monarchy
and his actual conspiratorial revolt is obvious, yet it cannot be
attributed to duplicity in Byron as a character. The root of the
contradiction is in the double level of his characterization: as a
humanized, naturalistic hero, he is inwardly divided; but, as a
political-moral principle in the dialectical conflict of the plot, he
is monolithic. As a man, he errs more and more as he subscribes
to false knowledge of the world and retreats from higher knowledge of himself; as an idea, he is a fixed embodiment of an erro-
neous position. Byron, like Bussy, fails to achieve inward as well
as outward virtù: not a fully realized man, he must function as

an object in this world, rather than as a subject. Simple *homo* is a mere tool of superior forces; only *homo spiritualis,* who mirrors the totality of the world, can transcend and command those forces.

After the speech on order, when Byron is informed of the King's command to return home from the threatened frontier where he has been stationed, his ego asserts itself in the downward direction of disorder. At first, he refuses to obey; later, he agrees to return—but for all of the wrong reasons. Warned that he will be in danger because the King knows of his treason, he interprets the challenging circumstance as a dare to his personal bravery; and, assured that La Fin has dispelled the King's doubts, he accepts the deceptive word of that corrupt politician and ignores the sincere misgivings of his other followers. Ruler and rebel meet coldly in an acid conversation that clearly reveals Byron's seething discontent.

The fourth act is ominously suspenseful: D'Auvergne observes that no one speaks to Byron or his friends, and the entire atmosphere at court is charged with foreboding. Soissons appears to give Byron a final warning and a chance to save himself by honest confession of his conspiratorial plans, but he stubbornly professes his innocence and his loyalty. A captain of the guard recites a gloomy portent: Postramo, Byron's horse, has killed himself, as did the favorite horse of the doomed traitor Essex the night before his execution. Byron grimly plays a polite game of primero with the Queen, while the troubled King leaves the room deep in thought, then returns abruptly, his mind made up:

> It is resolv'd; a work shall now be done,
> Which, while learn'd Atlas shall with stars be crown'd,
> While th' Ocean walks in storms his wavy round,
> While moons, at full, repair their broken rings,
> While Lucifer foreshows Aurora's springs,
> And Arctos sticks above the earth unmov'd,
> Shall make my realm be blest, and me belov'd. (IV, ii, 165–171)

But the magnanimous ruler gives the intransigent rebel one more chance to save himself by confession. Byron, however, simply asseverates his innocence. An effective use of dramaturgic contrast marks the scenes in which first Byron, then D'Auvergne, are arrested. Byron rages, exalting his sword hyperbolically as a symbol of the injustice done to a noble warrior:

> And take away sword;
> A proper point of force; ye had as good
> Have robb'd me of my soul, slaves of my stars
> Partial and bloody! O that in mine eyes
> Were all the sorcerous poison of my woes
> That I might witch ye headlong from your height,
> And trample out your execrable light. (IV, ii, 280–86)

D'Auvergne's submission to arrest, on the other hand, is quietly humorous:

> My sword? Who fears it? It was ne'er the death
> Of any but wild boars. I prithee take it;
> Hadst thou advertis'd, this when last we met,
> I had been in my bed, and fast asleep
> Two hours ago; lead, I'll go where thou wilt. (IV, ii, 298–302)

The homiletic juxtaposition is clear enough; but, when Epernon and Vidame comment epigrammatically on its obvious moral contrast, their words culminate in the favorite Chapman theme of the inner man: "his state still is best / That hath most inward worth" (IV, ii, 309–10).

The fifth act of the *Tragedy* is poetically as well as dramatically the most powerful of the entire epic drama. The focus moves away from King Henry, who speaks his final piece early in the act, to settle on Byron in his last hours. The contrast between Byron and D'Auvergne is strikingly betrayed in their prison behavior:

> One of them,
> Which is the Count D'Auvergne, hath merry spirits,
> Eats well and sleeps, and never can imagine
> That any place where he is, is a prison;
> Where, on the other part, the Duke Byron,
> Enter'd his prison as into his grave,
> Rejects all food, sleeps not, nor once lies down: (V, i, 102–8)

In the second scene the Chancellor reads the formal indictment of treason to Byron, who admits to only one specific charge: that of plotting with Count Fuentes against the realm, not so much in disloyalty as in sheer spite at King Henry for having deprived him of his hard-won citadel. When La Fin appears as a willing witness against him, Byron pleads that he was the victim of witchcraft. This curious episode was taken from Grimeston, who quoted Byron's actual charges against La Fin as one who had bewitched him. In his usual hyperbolic language, Byron then delivers a lengthy appeal in his own defense that so delays the judges that they postpone passing formal sentence on him.

Back in his cell, Byron mocks the Chancellor, parodying his legalistic language. Still blindly convinced of his inevitable acquittal, he arrogantly assumes that the king could not get along without him. When informed that the king does indeed wish his death, he is still confident enough of his own importance to expect clemency in return for an apology; but it is now too late. Boasting feverishly of his thirty-five wounds in the service of his country and protesting all the way, he capitulates reluctantly to the guard assigned to accompany him to his execution.

Epernon assumes a choral role to comment on the contradictory nature of the proud captive and of all men:

> Oh of what contraries consists a man!
> Of what impossible mixtures! Vice and virtue,
> Corruption and eternesse, at one time,
> And in one subject, let together loose!
> We have not any strength but weakens us,
> No greatness but doth crush us into air.
> Our knowledges do light us but to err,
> Our ornaments are burthens, our delights
> Are our tormentors, fiends that, rais'd in fears,
> At parting shake our roofs about our ears. (V, iii, 189–198)

Objective knowledge must be fallible in this sublunary world in which objects delude, men deceive, and actions betray. Subjective knowledge, however, although it may in effect illuminate our errors, also enables us to transcend them.

The human "contraries" mount in intensity in the final scene, which depicts the execution of the paradoxical Byron. Seemingly self-sufficient at last, he scorns the solace of a priest:

> Let me alone in peace.
> And leave my soul to me, whom it concerns;
> You have no charge of it; I feel her free:

> How she doth rouse and like a falcon stretch
> Her silver wings, as threatening Death with death;
> At whom I joyfully will cast her off. (V, iv, 26–31)

But, in a sudden surge of orthodoxy, he scorns the poor mortal body because of his traditional Christian view of death:

> I know this body but a sink of folly,
> The ground-work and rais'd frame of woe and frailty,
> The bond and bundle of corruption,
> A quick corse, only sensible of grief,
> A walking sepulchre, or household thief,
> A glass of air, broken with less than breath,
> A slave bound face to face to Death till death. (V, iv, 32–38)

Having abruptly moved from a worldly Renaissance individualism to a mood of medieval *contemptus mundi,* Byron then voices a typically seventeenth-century lament concerning life's darkness and futility:

> I know, besides,
> That life is but a dark and stormy night
> Of senseless dreams, terrors, and broken sleeps;
> A tyranny, devising pains to plague
> And make man long in dying, racks his death;
> And Death is nothing; what can you say more?
> I [being] a [large] globe, and a little earth,
> Am seated like earth, betwixt both the heavens,
> That if I rise, to heaven I rise; if fall,
> I likewise fall to heaven; what stronger faith
> Hath any of your souls? What say you more?
> Why lose I time in these things? Talk of knowledge!
> It serves for inward use. I will not die
> Like to a clergyman; but like the captain
> That pray'd on horseback, and with sword in hand,
> Threaten'd the sun, commanding it to stand;
> These are but ropes of sand. (V, iv, 39–55)

But his courageous words dissolve before the impact of the death sentence, which incites the doomed man to desperate imprecations. He threatens first to strangle the executioner, then half of the crowd of people present in order to force the other half to kill him. The Herculean fury is quickly spent, however, and Byron subdues his passion and dies with resigned dignity rather than in futile rage. Although he has ironically rejected knowledge since "it serves for inward use," he has nevertheless attained a larger perspective of human life, as evidenced by his final speech, which echoes the Preacher in Ecclesiastes:

> Such is the endless exile of dead men.
> Summer succeeds the Spring; Autumn the Summer;
> The frosts of Winter the fall'n leaves of Autumn:
> All these and all fruits in them yearly fade,
> And every year return: but cursed man
> Shall never more renew his vanish'd face. (V, iv, 247–52)

Like Bussy, Byron dies as on a purgatorial pyre that frees the noble spirit from the corrupting flesh; unlike Bussy, he is not free until the moment of death's violent emancipation but instead clings to the "natural" virtues of the active man.

The poetic style of both plays supports the heroic characterization of the embattled Byron and Henry. The dialogue surges relentlessly, incorporating epic similes, vivid metaphors, and exalting hyperbole. Even with the figurative and rhetorical embellishments, Chapman maintains a consistent level of clarity and directness in his language. But with Byron dies Chapman's Herculean hero; and, to a certain extent, the Herculean language fades as well. The next tragic protagonists were to be not so much heroic as saintly; not consumed by passion, they are sustained by wisdom.

CHAPTER 6

Senecal Saints

THE successors to Chapman's Herculean heroes are men of a different stamp; they are models of stoic virtue rather than militant individualists. Clermont (*The Revenge of Bussy*), Chabot (*The Tragedy of Chabot*), and Cato (*Caesar and Pompey*) are Senecal saints whose inner wisdom rules their outward actions and whose heroism is manifested in quiet endurance rather than in reckless defiance. Scholars who have mastered the art of living well, they achieve a poised indifference to life and death that enables them to live and to die with equal dignity. These tragic heroes are the descendants of the patiently suffering Odysseus rather than of the wrathful Achilles. Unlike Bussy and Byron, they gain genuine "wisdom," with a knowledge encompassing not merely nature but also *humanitas*. Fully realized rather than potential men, they have gained a high degree of freedom through inward virtue.

Exemplars of *homo spiritualis*, they function as both eye and mirror of the universe; but they do not merely receive images of things, they also create their own heroic forms.[1] Their mythical archetype (and that of Odysseus) is Prometheus, who took from the gods the all-illuminating fire in order to transform enslaved nature to liberated intellect. Their ethical mentor is Seneca, who, like Socrates, equated virtue with knowledge and who in his noble stoicism achieved a synthesis of the elements within man and a harmony between man and the universe.

Chapman's tragedies involving these three reflective heroes are different in tone and structure from those dominated by the active heroes. In a sense these plays are less stageworthy because they lack overt action and episodic pace. Their plots are dramatic, however, if not actually theatrical, in that they are structured dialectically about opposing themes. Often the action progresses by debate rather than through episode, and the relatively static plot develops vertically through illustration rather than horizontally through complication. Characterization in these plays is, for the most part, subordinated to the delineation of the protagonist. The poetry, although less flamboyant than that of the Bussy and Byron plays, is sustained on a high intellectual level and demands much from the reader.

I The Revenge of Bussy

Ostensibly a sequel to *Bussy D'Ambois*, *The Revenge of Bussy* is utterly different in form and technique from the earlier play and is also wholly unconventional as a revenge tragedy of its era. The revenger-hero Clermont is quite the opposite of the irate, passionate prototype of the revenger out for blood that had been so popular on the stage ever since Kyd's *Spanish Tragedy*.[2] Chapman achieved a new twist on the old theme by portraying a reluctant revenger who answers the call to honor from his brother's ghost with moral repugnance. And, throughout the play, his patience, poise, and philosophical purpose are contrasted with the more elemental revenge motives of Bussy's sister and with the primitive perturbations of several minor male characters. The play becomes in effect a monument to the "Senecal man," Clermont, who transcends revenge even as he executes it.

The opening scene parallels that of *Bussy* in its elegiac and satirical tone. Here the nostalgic lament is for the good old days when "things most lawful / Were once most royal" (I, i, 19–20). The figure of Baligny, later revealed as a despicable tool of royalty, attributes this decline to the slothfulness engendered by peace: deprived of the heroic challenge of battle, men turn their energies to ignoble pastimes such as getting money. The discussion turns from the general complaint to the specific wrong inflicted on the "brave," recently murdered Bussy D'Ambois. Baligny complains that his wife, Bussy's sister, will not leave him in peace until he avenges the victim. But the man destined for the deed is the rash Bussy's stoic brother, Clermont. And from his first appearance on stage, the play is dominated by the exemplary figure of Clermont, for other characters are placed on stage largely for purposes of contrast with him. A series of episodes, which seem static, display organically the overwhelming difference between the Senecal saint and the ordinary herd of mediocre men.

Monsieur first demonstrates Clermont's character by subjecting his renowned stoic temper to a test. Recalling his own exchange of rank insults with the fiery Bussy, Monsieur tries to taunt his brother into a similar exchange by a series of offensive remarks. Clermont remains calm until, after lightly parrying several insults, he coolly challenges Monsieur's kingly lineage as a mere accident that might have happened to any fool: "You did no princely deeds / Ere you're born, I take it, to deserve it; / Nor did you any since that I have heard; / Nor will do ever any, as all think" (I, i, 284–87). Clermont's knowledge of character is more sophisticated than the wily politician had suspected.

Next the equivocating and treacherous Baligny, who is juxtaposed to Clermont, egregiously flatters the king. Baligny justifies villainy committed in the name of kings as "truest loyalty" and denies that he would even dream of resorting to flattery. In contrast, Clermont's praise of the Guise is genuine, setting him off from those "painted men, All set on out-side," who within are "starv'd of mind" and have "a peasant's entrails." Baligny is obliged to confess to his meretricious diplomacy whereas the Guise can honestly praise his protégé Clermont:

> . . . because, besides his valour,
> He hath the crown of man, and all his parts,
> Which learning is; and that so true and virtuous
> That it gives power to do as well as say
> Whatever fits a most accomplish'd man;
> Which Bussy, for his valour's season, lack'd. (II, i, 83–89)

When the action shifts from the court to the castle at Cambrai, where Baligny's officers receive letters from King Henry ordering Clermont's arrest, the contrasting reactions expressed provide choral commentary on the situation. The cynical Maillard scoffingly explains: "It is Virtue's fortune, / To keep her low, and in her proper place; / Height hath no room for her" (III, i, 28–30). But Aumale, puzzled at the uncharacteristic involvement in political intrigue which the arrest seems to imply, seeks a more philosophical explanation in the fact of Bussy's sin, which has tainted the entire family.

Clermont is then sharply contrasted with his sister Charlotte, whose fiery temperament blazes futilely around his impregnable fortress of restraint. This "manly sister," a veritable virago, seethes with a passionate desire for immediate vengeance. She taunts and mocks "bungling, foggy-spirited men" in general and her brother-in-law in particular for delaying the act of revenge. Clermont finally permits himself to castigate her, in his own quietly ironic way, by suggesting that she attend to her cosmetics and leave the revenge to him. The impetuous Charlotte, who does not for a moment believe the warning about Maillard's treachery which she receives in an anonymous letter, dismisses it as a "mere bugbear."

Clermont's integrity is then poised against the rank Machiavellianism of Maillard, who has no scruples to restrain him from the perjury of a false oath, a profane lie. Although Clermont's intuition warns him to distrust Maillard, his stoic integrity demands that he honor his oath. He then accompanies Maillard into what turns out to be a trap. Unperturbed by the treachery, Clermont lectures Maillard on the importance of inner control in men of renown, citing the negative example of Achilles:

> When Homer made Achilles passionate,
> Wrathful, revengeful, and insatiate
> In his affections, what man will deny
> He did compose it all of industry,
> To let men see that men of most renown,
> Strong'st, noblest, fairest, if they set not down
> Decrees within them, for disposing these,
> Of judgment, resolution, uprightness,
> And certain knowledge of their use and ends,
> Mishap and misery no less extends
> To their destruction, with all that they priz'd,
> Than to the poorest, and the most despis'd. (III, iv, 14–25)

Maillard, who denies any guilt in his lie, declares that to forswear for the King is not at all dishonest. That Clermont cannot understand this obvious fact means that he is no politician. Nor is he a lawyer, for he naïvely insists that things do not change when the terms applied to them are bandied about. Clermont will submit to arrest but not before aiming some sharp language at this offensive dealer in "false policy." Even then his submission to Maillard is no mere acquiescence: he turns "wild lightening," scattering soldiers about the field like autumn leaves. But, once

captured, he voices his stoic disdain for the vicissitudes of fortune; he prefers to "sway with" the universe rather than rebel
against its malevolence, as did his ill-fated brother. In the mood
of Epictetus, Clermont explains:

> That in this one thing, all the discipline
> Of manners and of manhood is contain'd:
> A man to join himself with th'Universe
> In his main sway, and make (in all things fit)
> One with that All, and go on round as it;
> Not plucking from the whole his wretched part,
> And into straits, or into nought revert,
> Wishing the complete Universe might be
> Subject to such a rag of it as he;
> But to consider great Necessity
> All things as well refract as voluntary
> Reduceth to the prime celestial cause;
> Which he that yields to with a man's applause,
> And cheek by cheek goes, crossing it no breath,
> But, like God's image, follows to the death,
> That man is truly wise, and everything
> (Each cause, and every part distinguishing)
> In nature with enough art understands,
> And that full glory merits at all hands,
> That doth the whole world at all parts adorn,
> And appertains to one celestial born. (IV, i, 137–57)

Although not quite so stoically resigned, the Countess of Cambrai proves a worthy mistress to the stout-hearted Clermont. Her
reaction to the news of his arrest is both spirited and rational:
she attacks the King's role as corrupt, intimating the potential
threat to a kingdom under such a rule, and then asserts her own
courageous stand against the conspiracy, vowing never to die
until she has personally given Maillard a hundred slashes with
a sword. Her self-control yields under pressure, however; loss
of her Senecal saint eventually leads her to weep herself blind
with grief.

The business of Clermont's arrest, which occupies the middle
acts of the play, is wound up when the king learns that the
"machiavellian villains" are responsible for the charge of treason
and promptly gives order for Clermont's release. Unmoved by the
change in events, the hero asserts toward his promised release the

same indifference that he had displayed toward his unjust seizure.

The ghost conventionally expected in a revenge play appears late in the action and without any of the sensational trappings traditionally associated with such apparitions. Although the Guise is present during the nocturnal visitation, only Clermont perceives it. The spirit does not neglect to direct polite amenities to the unseeing but perturbed Guise who, for his original role in the murder, has reason to fear the invisible guest. The shade of Bussy then delivers his urgent communication without fanfare, and the reluctant revenger agrees to do his duty. Meanwhile, the spirited Charlotte, whose sulphurous passion cannot abide Clermont's reasoned delay, has donned male attire in her determination to effect the revenge with her own hands. But, when she bursts in upon the confrontation of Clermont and the guilty Montsurry, husband of Tamyra, impulsively volunteering to finish off the culprit, her brother scorns her into momentary patience as he fulfills the grim deed himself.

As for Montsurry, who has abjectly refused to fight for his life until prodded by Clermont, he is restored to nobility in his death as he generously forgives all concerned and breaks Tamyra's heart with poignant regrets. The poised tranquillity of this moment of resolution is interrupted, however, by the harsh news of the death of the Guise. This worthy man is a victim of King Henry, who feared his ambition and ordered an ambush to remove a potential threat to his power. Clermont recognizes at once that this time revenge cannot assuage the evil fact: "There's no disputing with the acts of kings, / Revenge is impious on their sacred persons" (V, v, 151–152). But neither can he accept the separation from his friend, which he likens to the schism of body and soul. Alone, he calmly resolves to follow the Guise rather than to continue "to feed thieves, beasts, and be the slave of power" (V, v, 192).

Clermont, who in his superior learning, insists upon the distinction between men and beasts, prefers death to life in a world where "souls are smother'd in the flatter'd flesh." Firm in knowledge of himself as well as of the world, his choice is clear. Somewhat below him in wisdom, as in resolve, are the female characters who conclude the play with a choral lament. The virile Charlotte, passionately approving her brother's heroic decision to commit suicide, resolves to leave the weak Baligny; the now

blind Countess, wishing her life to follow her eyes to darkness,
awaits death; and Tamyra, woefully repentant, plans to retire
to the cloister.

Superior though he is, Clermont is the least attractive of Chapman's tragic heroes. His stoic decision for suicide does not engage
the reader's sympathy, as does that of either Chabot or Cato.
And the gnomic wisdom of his Senecan speeches, however admirable objectively, fails to involve the reader who has his own
personal convictions. Chapman's episodic pageant of a saintly
hero moving stiffly through encounters with inferior worldlings
is poetically successful but dramatically disappointing.

Occasionally the language breathes fire like its predecessor, as
when Tamyra recalls her dead lover, Bussy:

> O Earth, why keep'st thou not as well his spirit
> To give his form life? No, that was not earthly;
> That (rarefying the thin and yielding air)
> Flew sparkling up into the sphere of fire,
> Whence endless flames it sheds in my desire:
> Here be my daily pallet; here all nights
> That can be wrested from thy rival's arms,
> O my dear Bussy, I will lie and kiss
> Spirit into thy blood, or breathe out mine
> In sighs, and kisses, and sad tunes to thine. (I, ii, 15–24)

And, although for the most part the dialogue is rhetorical rather
than metaphorical, it is heightened by epic similes, as in Clermont's death scene:

> . . . .   Now, then, as a ship,
> Touching at strange and far-removed shores,
> Her men ashore go, for their several ends,
> Fresh water, victuals, precious stones, and pearl,
> All yet intentive (when the master calls,
> The ship to put off ready) to leave all
> Their greediest labours, lest they there be left
> To thieves or beasts, or be the country's slaves:
> So, now my master calls, my ship, my venture,
> All in one bottom put, all quite put off,
> Gone under sail, and I left negligent,
> To all the horrors of the vicious time,
> The far-removed shores to all virtuous aims,

None favouring goodness, none but he respecting
Piety or manhood—shall I here survive,
Not cast me after him into the sea,
Rather than here live, ready every hour
To feed thieves, beasts, and be the slave of power?
I come, my lord! Clermont, thy creature, comes. (V, v, 175–93)

On the whole, however, the elegant language is static, and fine long speeches are not enlivened by simultaneous action. In fact, this one play seems to justify the traditional disparagement of Chapman's theatricality: Clermont's "most gentle and unwearied mind / Rightly to virtue fram'd" leaves one nostalgic for the flamboyant Bussy.

II The Tragedy of Chabot, Admiral of France

Chapman's last play based on French history, *The Tragedy of Chabot*, was not published during his lifetime. It was entered in the Stationers' Register in 1638 and published in 1639, with the dual authorship of Chapman and James Shirley listed on the title page. Although nothing definite is known about its stage history, except for the reference on the title page to the performance by Her Majesties Servants, Shirley's company, it is usually assumed that the play was originally written by Chapman for his own company, the Queens Revels, and then transferred from it to the Princess Elizabeth's men, with whom this company united in 1613 and with whom it remained after it took the name of Her Majesties Servants in 1625. Scholars have been almost unanimous in agreeing that the play was originally written entirely by Chapman and only retouched by Shirley after the older poet's death.[3] Both the sententious, long speeches and the elaborate similes are trademarks of Chapman's style; and the tone of the dialogue, always heavy and occasionally turgid, suggests Chapman rather than the facile hand of Shirley. With the exception of the expanded female roles, which suggest Shirley rather than the older dramatist, the play may be considered as Chapman's.

The source of the tragedy was Etienne Pasquier's *Les Recherches de la France*[4] with its account of Philipe de Chabot, intimate friend and advisor of King Francis I. The recipient of many honors and titles, Chabot had aroused the rivalry of another favorite of Francis, Anne de Montmorency, who exploited the munificent mode of Admiral de Chabot's living to charge him with defrauding the royal treasury. Chabot's proud profession of innocence to Francis only infuriated the arrogant monarch, who promptly threw him into prison and ordered him to be tried by Chancellor Poyet, who managed to fabricate twenty-five charges against the Admiral, only two of which were substantiated in court. Poyet revised the relatively minor sentence passed on Chabot, however, by adding "for life" to the unspecified term of banishment. One of the outraged judges, signing only under duress, faintly wrote in the letters "vi" to expose the forced signature of the document. As the result of a personal appeal by Francis' wife, who championed Chabot, the sentence was revoked; and shortly after the injustice of the trial was revealed. Conniving Chancellor Poyet was sent to the Bastille for his ignominious role in the proceedings; and Chabot, although pardoned, never recovered from the experience and died shortly thereafter.

The obvious ethical implications of the account naturally appealed to Chapman, who also saw in it a more immediate significance. In the fraudulent trial of a virtuous man and his manifestly unfair conviction by unscrupulous men of policy, Chapman recognized a close analogy to the recent case involving his patron, Robert Carr, the Earl of Somerset, tried for the murder of Thomas Overbury. As Mrs. Solve demonstrated,[5] Chapman's tragedy not only relates French history but is also a clearly topical allegory of the recent, sensational English case involving Somerset and resulting subsequently in the exposure and downfall of Chancellor Bacon. In this political allegory, Admiral Chabot represents the loyal but highly independent Somerset; King Francis, his equally vain counterpart James; and the Queen, whose shifting allegiance was so central in the Chabot case, Queen Anne. Poyet, the Chancellor, is a highly satirical but accurate version of the brilliant but expedient and meretricious Bacon. The Advocate, whose brutal invective and savage temper shamed the court, reflects the notorious Sir Edward Coke. The affable Montmorency closely resembles the popular George Villiers; and the Treasurer and Secretary represent, respectively, Sir Henry Montague and Sir Ralph Winwood.

The tragedy opens, as did The Revenge, with an attack on the present "vile, degenerate age" in which a "good man" like the Admiral, current favorite of the king, is threatened by competition from a new favorite who is merely a "great man"—Montmorency, the Constable. The moral lines of force are established, and the unimpeachable integrity of Chabot is opposed to the easily swayed opinions of the pliable Constable and to the ugly voice of policy speaking through the Chancellor. The crucial figure at the center of the conflict is King Francis, an able but authoritarian monarch whose judgments are more political than profound. Choric commentary is provided by Chabot's father-in-law, who has long scorned the corruption of court life and who appears now only in response to disturbing rumors of a new favorite usurping his son-in-law's honored role. In the presence of his father-in-law Chabot receives for signature a state bill, which he angrily tears when he discerns its unjust contents, thereby inflaming the king's resentment.

In a brilliant debate between King Francis and Chabot, the principles of absolute monarchy and individual integrity clash in open conflict over the theme of justice. Once more the ultimate issue is knowledge. The King, whose knowledge is limited to the level of policy, is convinced that politically successful men, however honestly motivated, must have resorted to base political means. Consequently, he not only distrusts Chabot's avowal that his honors and riches mean nothing to him but also rejects the proposition that, since the rewards were for merit, they imply no inherent obligation to the king who granted them. When the offended monarch rises in anger to order an immediate trial for this obvious "traitor," Chabot dispassionately warns the king of the danger lurking in flattering, fraudulent counselors, whom he has learned to disdain as "grave toys I shall despise in death" (II, iii, 151).

In the meantime Chabot's wife and her father prepare to face the Queen. The wife humbly kneels to the approaching monarch, who, however, greets her with words of undisguised sarcasm. The father, who cannot submit to such insolence, however regal, speaks in protest:

> I must confess
> I am a man out of this element,
> No courtier; yet I am a gentleman
> That dare speak honest truth to the Queen's ear
> (A duty every subject wo'not pay you),
> And justify it to all the world. (III, i, 98–101)

Montmorency praises the "brave old man," and the wife now asserts herself as she professes her own innocence of that pride the queen has attributed to her, and courageously dares to "forgive" that haughty ruler. Although the queen is momentarily angry, she is gradually won over by the courage and heroic integrity of the woman arguing her husband's loyalty: "I sooner will suspect the stars may lose / Their way, and crystal heaven return to chaos; / Truth sits not on her square more firm than he" (III, i, 189–91). Like Montmorency, who admits that he is caught up in a conspiracy conceived by others—"not that / My own will would incline me" (III, i, 222–23)—the queen realizes that she has been misled by gossip about Admiral Chabot and his wife.

In sharp dramaturgic contrast, the scene in the court of justice reveals the hypocrisy and virulence of the Proctor-General in action: his address of accusation moves from specious flattery to egregious insult. Even the Chancellor, whom he grossly flatters, voices impatience with his prolix oratory. Actually, the long, vehement tirade includes only one specific charge against the Admiral—the unfair taxation on some Normandy fishermen; but the Chancellor makes sweeping claims of unmentioned "disloyalties, infidelities, contempts, oppressions, extortions, with innumerable abuses, offences, and forfeits" (III, ii, 101–3). Such vilification had made the court speeches of Sir Edward Coke notorious. When the judges sensibly dismiss the minor charge of tax exaction as unworthy of the major punishments recommended by the Advocate they are threatened by the Chancellor and forced to sign the conviction.

When Chabot's conviction is reported, the Constable and the Queen join the father-in-law and the wife in an attempt to move the King to pardon the hapless Admiral. But King Francis reveals in a soliloquy that he is toying with the tense situation. Rather like Byron, who wished to destroy France in order to revive her, he intends to refuse a pardon temporarily in order to give the greater impression of mercy when he finally grants it. Swollen in arrogance and confident in his cunning, the King stages his change of heart melodramatically:

> therefore,
> By that most absolute power, with which all right
> Puts in my hands these issues, turns, and changes,
> I here, in ear of all these, pardon all

> Your faults and forfeits, whatsoever censur'd,
> Again advancing and establishing
> Your person in all fulness of that state
> That ever you enjoy'd before th'attainder. (IV, i, 221–24)

But as the exclamations of praise and relief pour forth and then subside, a moment of silence ensues, and Chabot speaks quietly: "You cannot pardon me, sir" (IV, i, 234). Firm in his conviction, the Admiral explains that to accept a pardon would be equivalent to confessing guilt: an innocent man cannot be pardoned. He succeeds in persuading King Francis to send for the judges in order to hear directly from them the extent of his supposed crimes. Although the Chancellor has been summoned with them, they admit to their sovereign that the decision for conviction was arrived at under duress, and is therefore unbinding in law; and they also explain the incriminating "vi" which they had inserted after the Chancellor's threats forced them to sign the bill. The Chancellor mutters that he is undone, and the irate King, suddenly aware of the whole conspiracy, orders his immediate arrest.

But justice is still a mere word in this court in which genuine learning is out of place. The brave Admiral, subjected to the disillusionment of King Francis' attack on his integrity, has not rallied from his conviction and subsequent pardon but, crushed in spirit, has wasted away. An interview with his faithful servant Allegre, tortured on the rack until unable to walk, also dissipates his desire to live. The touching encounter of these two men of high integrity—one crushed spiritually, the other physically—ironically confirms the father-in-law's satiric description of perversion and corruption of the court.

The theme of justice is amplified through a second trial scene.[6] A dramatically effective anti-trial, that contradicts the fraudulence of the earlier one but maintains the virulent Advocate in his same hypocritical role, puts an end to the Chancellor's career. To the Advocate, the very man whom he had earlier exalted as "poet" and "creator" is now "this odious and polluted chancellor, a man of so tainted and contagious a life that it is a miracle any man enjoyeth his nostrils that has lived within the scent of his offices." Poyet escapes with removal from office and a heavy fine (the same sentence inflicted on Chancellor Bacon), despite the call for blood from the fickle crowd aroused against him.

Ironically, however, although the convicted Chancellor escapes death, the pardoned Chabot succumbs, inflicting a death sentence on himself. His spirit shattered by the unjust proceedings against him, he loses his vital strength and submits to death. Before he dies, he sees King Francis again, in time to hear a genuine eulogy from his sovereign's lips: "He has a victory in's death; this world / Deserv'd him not. How soon he was translated / To glorious eternity! 'Tis too late / To fright the air with words; my tears embalm him!" (V, iii, 206–9). Chabot, like Clermont, abdicates a world unworthy of his ideals. A truly learned man, he has the inner fortitude to regard life and death with equal indifference and the wisdom to abandon the toys of worldliness for the sake of the eternal verities. His virtue disqualifies him for continued life in this world of policy and cynicism, but his departure from it is a victory, not a surrender.

III   The Tragedy of Caesar and Pompey

Chapman's least-known tragedy, *The Tragedy of Caesar and Pompey,* has suffered critical neglect because of its very corrupt text and because of unfortunate comparison of it with other plays on the same subject. Contemporary criticism, which varies widely in its estimate of the play, ranges from defense of its effectiveness[7] to scorn of its "hurly-burly." [8] Scholarly estimates of its date also vary considerably, ranging from the long accepted view that it is Chapman's latest play, written about 1612,[9] to the opposing view propounded recently that it is an early play, dating back to about 1605.[10] The playwright himself contributed to the factual confusion in a dedication, dated 1631, in which he admits to the much earlier composition of the play ("written so long since") and apparently without subsequent revision: "I yet find no fault withal for any such defects."

A strong piece of factual evidence favoring the earlier dating is the reference in *Northward Ho* to a play about Caesar and Pompey written by Bellamont, who is almost certainly intended as a portrait of Chapman. Establishing the earlier date, however, only opens the larger question of what happened to the play between its composition and its publication in 1631. Here again the author further clouds the picture by announcing in the dedication that "though . . . this martial history suffer the division of acts and scenes, both for the more perspicuity and height of the celebration, yet never touched it at the stage"; but, as a play, it is remarkable for its elaborate stage directions.

The argument with which the author prefixes the play manifests its homiletic purpose: to illustrate the theme that "Only a just man is a free man." The tragedy is thus more overtly didactic than is usual even with Chapman. The unity of the play is accordingly analogical, in the medieval mode. The polarities of justice and injustice are demonstrated together with an exploration of intermediate gradations. Caesar and Cato are introduced in the opening action at opposite moral extremes, with Pompey in the middle. Caesar, the pure Machiavellian, is calculating and unscrupulous in fulfilling his worldly ambitions. On the other hand, Cato, the Senecal saint, has such devotion to integrity and such an indifference to the world that he overshadows even Clermont and Chabot. Pompey, the focal character of the action in that he alone changes, is divided in his extreme admiration for both men. The play then develops the theme of freedom through justice by thematic variants displayed through these three disparate characters.

The tragedy opens with Cato's exposition of the "two suns of our Roman heaven," whose contention threatens all Rome. His own determination to save his city is not at all diminished by the slight chance for success: "I know it," he says to a follower, "yet let us do like ourselves" (I, i, 95). In the subsequent scene at the Forum, Cato courageously speaks up in favor of admitting Pompey's army "since, I as well think, he affects not th'Empire" (I, ii, 134), but he is against admission of Caesar's forces, a collective symbol of his personal ambition. Pompey, who also speaks forthrightly, asserts his triumph over three continents and disdains the partiality of Fortune—"Though some have said she was the page of Caesar" (I, ii, 167). Pompey's language reflects Chapman's personal antipathy as he castigates the "gilded" speeches of Caesar: "You speak well, and are learn'd; and golden speech / Did Nature never give man but to gild / A copper soul in him; and all that learning / That heartily is spent in painting speech, / Is merely painted, and no solid knowledge" (I, ii, 236–40). And he moralizes Caesar's notorious illnesses as a divine scourge: "The gods inflict on men diseases never, / Or other outward maims,

but to decipher / Correct, and order some rude vice within them"
(I, ii, 260–62). The act ends with the angry crowd divided between the two lines of force so clearly explicated to them.

The somewhat puzzling opening scene of the second act introduces a typically Elizabethan comic inversion of the main action;
what is perplexing about it is not its inclusion, for it is a conventional enough device, but rather its uniqueness in this play, for
the characters of Fronto, the ragged soldier, and the devil, Ophioneus, never return to the stage. Fronto, a villainous rogue fed
up with the inconveniences of war, offers to hang himself in de-
spair. His cowardly attempt at suicide is thwarted by the sudden,
spectacular appearance of Ophioneus, a medieval devil "with the
face, wings, and tail of a dragon: a skin coat all speckled on the
throat," who reminds Fronto of the infinite opportunities for villainy made possible by the war. The devil's lines incorporate a
satirical point of view on the current Roman scene, and Fronto,
enormously cheered by this grim exposition of a world in which
the greatest criminals receive the highest rewards, takes the path
to similar achievement.

The devil's pessimistic vision is echoed by the messenger's
account of fear and chaos spreading throughout Rome. But in
the Pompeian camp Cato advises the triumphant leader to spare
lives, to sack no cities, and to subject no Roman citizen to the
sword. Cato himself, dispatched by the Senate to survey "the
cities and the kingdoms situate / About your either army" (II,
iv, 64–65), undertakes the mission with no misgivings about the
ominous storm raging at the time of his departure. For the superstitious Caesar, however, "The wrathful tempest of the angry
night . . . / Hath rous'd the Furies, arm'd in all their horrors"
(II, v. 1, 5). Although a former minion of Fortune, he generously
exonerates Fortune from blame for his failure: "It was not Fortune's fault, but mine" (II, iii, 10). Pompey, on the other hand,
conjures Fortune into his own ranks:

> so may Fortune now,
> The flood of all our enemy's forces passing
> With her fair ensigns, and arriv'd at ours,
> Displume her shoulders, cast off her wing'd shoes,
> Her faithless and still-rolling stone spurn from her,
> And enter our powers, as she may remain
> Our firm assistant. (II, iv, 136–42)

But, as pride and overconfidence overcome his better judgment, Pompey departs from the wise Cato's advice and urges an attack on Caesar's forces. Caesar, having consulted a soothsayer who reports encouraging omens, resolves on his part to give battle to Pompey. He exults in the opportunity for martial action: "I rejoice to see / This long-time-look'd-for and most happy day, / In which we now shall fight, with men, not hunger" (III, ii, 92–94).

Pompey, who suffered outward defeat when he neglected Cato's advice, returns, through subsequent inward suffering, to a heightened awareness of the wisdom inherent in Cato's words. Torturing himself with reproaches, he resolves to fly to Cato, pausing on the way to comfort his wife and children. In his journey, he also moves toward a stoic position: "But now 'tis helpless, and no cause in me, / Rest in these embers my unmoved soul / With any outward change, this distich minding; / 'No man should more allow his own loss woes, / (Being past his fault) than any stranger does'" (IV, iii, 71–75). The victorious Caesar is also suffering: he witnesses the needless slaughter with profound regret, and he receives the disturbing news that the two consuls have committed suicide. Ironically, Caesar also plans to see Cato and prays that "His love may strengthen my success to-day" (IV, iv, 47).

The tragedy culminates with the focus on Cato. At his house in Utica, Cato's son fears for his father's life when he discovers a sword hanging by the bed. Cato, who appears on stage in a scholarly pose, book in hand, anticipates expression of the misgiving which he detects in the faces of his son and friends by introducing himself the subject of death. His intellectual position is paradoxical: man may enlarge life through death. His philosophical justification for suicide then culminates in a thoroughly Christian argument for immortality. Chapman's ideological loyalties, stoicism and Christianity, meet in this fervent speech of Cato's. Since life itself is subordinate to justice, death may mean freedom from injustice:

> she not destroys it
> When she dislives it, that their freedoms may
> Go firm together, like their powers and organs,
> Rather than let it live a rebel to her,
> Profaning that divine conjunction

> 'Twixt her and it; nay, a disjunction making
> Betwixt them worse than death, in killing quick
> That which in just death lives: being dead to her,
> If to her rule dead; and to her alive,
> If dying in her just rule. (V, v, 80–89)

Then the newly freed body may be rejoined to the soul:

> And therefore the mortality to which
> A man is subject rather is a sleep
> Than bestial death, since Sleep and Death are call'd
> The twins of Nature. For if absolute death
> And bestial seize the body of a man,
> Then is there no proportion in his parts,
> His soul being free from death, which otherwise
> Retains divine proportion. For as sleep
> No disproportion holds with human souls,
> But aptly quickens the proportion
> 'Twixt them and bodies, making bodies fitter
> To give up forms to souls, which is their end:
> So death (twin-born of sleep), resolving all
> Man's body's heavy parts, in lighter nature
> Makes a reunion with the spritely soul,
> When, in a second life their beings given,
> Holds their proportion firm in highest heaven. (IV, v, 107–23)

The familial scene in the domicile of Cato is contrapuntal to the domestic reunion on the island of Lesbos where Cornelia awaits her husband Pompey. Both the setting of the events which follow and Cornelia's character represent Chapman's own adaptation of history for the sake of dramatic effect. Pompey, returning from his defeat on the battlefield, has disguised himself for his appearance before his wife. He engages her in conversation about her "great" husband in order to discover whether she would welcome him as a fallen hero. In this intellectually sophisticated dialogue, she proves herself a witty "philosophress"; and, when he reveals himself ("I am cheerfully fallen; be cheerful", V, i, 159–160), she responds warmly, "I am, and welcome, as the world were clos'd / In these embraces" (V, i, 161–62). This ennobled portrait of Cornelia—who according to history was emotionally devastated by her husband's return and swooned rather than philosophized—enriches Chapman's gallery of high-minded heroines. The scene also reinforces one of Chapman's favorite themes: the conflict of goodness and greatness—

> Cor: O, Pompey, Pompey, never 'Great' till now!
> Pom: O, my Cornelia, let us still be good,
> And we shall still be great; and greater far
> In every solid grace than when the tumour
> And bile of rotten observation swell'd us.
> Griefs for wants outward are without our cure,
> Greatness, not of itself, is never sure. (V, i, 180–86)

Pompey's career comes full circle. After having drifted away from the stoic wisdom of Cato and after suffering bitter outward defeat, he places primary value on the world within:

> I will stand no more
> On others' legs, nor build one joy without me.
> If ever I be worth a house again
> I'll build all inward; not a light shall ope
> The common outway; no expense, no art,
> No ornament, no door will I use there,
> But raise all plain and rudely, like a rampier
> Against the false society of men
> That still batters
> All reason piecemeal, and, for earthy greatness,
> All heavenly comforts rarefies to air.
> I'll therefore live in dark, and all my light,
> Like ancient temples, let in at my top.
> This were to turn one's back to all the world,
> And only look at heaven. (V, i, 203–17)

At this peak of philosophical awareness of the supremacy of inner worth, Pompey is deprived of his outer self by soldiers who seize and murder him.

The transition to Cato's house, where that scholarly man is engrossed in study, is dramatically effective. He has just noticed that his sword is missing and sends a servant to fetch it. The servant fails, however, to return; and, after several members of Cato's household refuse the ominous errand, an innocent page, a mere boy, undertakes to bring the weapon to him. After rehearsing with Socratic calm and care the reasons for suicide, Cato falls on his sword:

No one thought of the world: I go each minute
Discharg'd of all cares that may fit my freedom.
The next world and my soul, then, let me serve
With her last utterance, that my body may
With sweetness of the passage drown the sour
That death will mix with it: the Consuls' souls,
That slew themselves so nobly, scorning life
Led under tyrants' sceptres, mine would see.
For we shall know each other, and past death
Retain those forms of knowledge learn'd in life;
Since, if what here we learn, we there shall lose,
Our immortality were not life, but time.
And that our souls in reason are immortal
Their natural and proper objects prove;
Which immortality and knowledge are. (V, ii, 129–43)

Not the most dramatically effective of Chapman's tragedies, *Caesar and Pompey* is an introspective play with integrity and clarity of meaning. Structured analogically on clear-cut Elizabethan lines, with skilled use of dramaturgic contrast, it may well be an earlier rather than a later play. In any event, Cato is one of Chapman's most exemplary heroes. In contrast to both Caesar and Pompey, with their shrewd political knowledge and shallow worldliness, he possesses genuine wisdom of both himself and the inner meanings of people and events. His learning is inseparable from his way of life; his soul both seeks and is knowledge. His last words confirm the thesis of the play that only the just are free; his last deed is a gesture of the highest freedom.

The poetry of the play is often fine, but not exciting. Lacking the metaphorical brilliance of *Bussy D'Ambois* and the Byron plays, it is stylistically closer to *Chabot* and *The Revenge*. And, although much more uneven than these plays in its rhetorical power, certain scenes display the same forcefulness and epic sweep, as when Cato courageously faces death:

O how men grudge, and shake, and fear, and fly
His stern approaches; all their comforts taken
In faith and knowledge of the bliss and beauties
That watch their wakings in an endless life,
Drown'd in the pains and horrors of their sense

Sustain'd but for an hour! Be all the earth
Rapt with this error, I'll pursue my reason,
And hold that as my light and fiery pillar,
Th'eternal law of heaven and earth no firmer. (V, ii, 36–44)

CHAPTER 7

Chapman Revaluated

UNFORTUNATELY, Chapman has never been neglected long
enough by the critics to occasion a fresh revaluation. Acknowledged as an important figure in his own time, he has continued to engage the attention of major critics in each succeeding
century. Acclaimed by his contemporary Francis Meres[1] as one
of the best writers of the time in both tragedy and comedy, he
has remained in dominant twentieth-century views among those
playwrights and poets who rank next to Shakespeare and Donne.
A survey of scholarly opinion of Chapman, however, reveals, on
the one hand, a striking similarity in the consensus of his faults
and, on the other, considerable differentiation in the enumeration
of his merits. In fact, one pervasive weakness of the criticism of
Chapman has been the perennial unanimity as to a certain few
faults, although a wide variety of compliments has been inspired
by his diversified merits.

Although Chapman has not been ignored, he has been consistently oversimplified. A highly complex, many-sided writer, he
has been subjected to a series of single, partial views. As a poet,
he has been likened in turn to figures as different as Edmund
Spenser and John Donne, Dante and Milton, Pope and Yeats.
Chapman is indeed like each of these poets, but only when
viewed from the narrow perspective of a single window. As a
dramatist, he has been traditionally regarded as a reluctant captive of the theater, as a proud poet unwillingly and unskillfully
channeling his verse through the vulgar medium of the stage.
His theatrical successes appeared, therefore, to be both acci-
dental and exceptional. These simplistic interpretations charac-
terize the history of Chapman criticism, which reveals many
illuminating insights into individual works but no comprehensive
and balanced view of his whole career.

I *Past Views*

Chapman did not fare well among the neo-Classic writers of the late seventeenth century, who were for the most part too shocked by what seemed to them the romantic excesses of *Bussy d'Ambois* to read any farther. Dryden, in his Dedication to the *Spanish Friar* (1681), attacked Chapman with the myopic vision and vituperative verve that distinguished Rymer's objections to *Othello:*

I have sometimes wondered, in the reading, what was become of those glaring colours which amazed me in *Bussy D'Amboys* upon the theatre; but when I had taken up what I supposed a fallen star, I found I had been cozened with a jelly; nothing but a cold, dull mass, which glittered no longer than it was shooting; a dwarfish thought, dressed up in gigantic words, repetition in abundance, looseness of expression, and gross hyperboles; the sense of one line expanded prodigiously into ten; and, to sum up all, uncorrect English, and a hideous mingle of false poetry, and true nonsense; or, at best, a scantling of wit, which lay gasping for life, and groaning beneath a heap of rubbish. A famous modern poet used to sacrifice every year a Statius to Virgil's *Manes;* and I have indignation enough to burn a D'Amboys annually to the memory of Jonson.[2]

Dryden's reaction to the Homeric translations was scarcely less scornful. Whatever pleasure the reader experienced, he explained, "must needs proceed from the author himself; for the translator has thrown him down as low as harsh numbers, improper English, and a monstrous length of verse could carry him." [3]

The Romantic temperament reacted much more favorably toward Chapman, as it did toward the Elizabethans in general. Early in the eighteenth century Thomas Warton praised the translations of Homer as worthy of Homeric approval; later Coleridge added his enthusiastic encomiums for both epics, although he personally preferred the *Odyssey*. Charles Lamb, enlightened beyond his contemporaries in lauding Chapman's plays rather than his poems, compared him with Shakespeare for the wrong reasons. Overlooking their analogous dramaturgy, he designated Chapman the one who, "of all the English playwriters, perhaps approaches nearest to Shakespeare in the descriptive and didactic, in passages which are less purely dramatic." He even forgave him his "unconquerable quaintness" for the sake of his verbal passion, capable of "raising the low, dignifying the mean, and putting sense into the absurd." [4] Although virtually nothing is known about Shelley's opinion of Chapman, his use of a passage from the earlier poet for an epitaph to one of his own poems indicates at least an interest.[5] And perhaps Chapman's Homer opened a new world to others than the youthful Keats.

Although the Victorians were more critical than the Romantics, they paid Chapman the compliment of lengthy commentary. Both Thomas Hazlitt and Matthew Arnold were severe. Arnold, in his essay on the art of translating Homer,[6] objected to the ornate complexity of the Jacobean version: ". . . the Elizabethan poet fails to render Homer because he cannot forbear to interpose a play of thought between his object and its expression. Chapman translates his object into Elizabethan." Usually so astute, Arnold betrayed his own limitation in failing to recognize the special value of precisely such a translation, not merely into the English language, but into the extraordinarily flexible and vital idiom of the heroic Elizabethan era.

The most acute and the most thorough of the many Victorian critics of Chapman was Swinburne, who contributed a long essay[7] and a sonnet to the history of Chapman scholarship.[8] His is in fact the only comprehensive study of Chapman before the twentieth century, and he was the first major critic to take the dramas seriously. Though essentially laudatory, his approach was by no means uncritical:

There are few poets from whose remains a more copious and noble anthology of detached beauties might be selected. He has a singular force and depth of moral thought, a constant energy and intensity of expression, an occasional delicacy and perfection of fanciful or reflective beauty, which should have ensured him a place in the front rank at least of gnomic poets. It is true that his "wisdom entangles itself in overniceness;" that his philosophy is apt to lose its way among brakes of digression and jungles of paradox; that his subtle and sleepless ingenuity can never resist the lure of any quaint or perverse illustration which may start across its path from some obscure corner at the unluckiest and unlikeliest time; that the rough and barren byways of incongruous allusion, of unreasonable reflection or preposterous and grotesque symbolism, are more tempting to his feet than the highway of art, and the brushwood or the morass of metaphysics seems often preferable in his eyes to the pastures or the gardens of poetry. But from first to last the grave and frequent blemishes of his genius bear manifestly more likeness to the deformities of a giant than to the malformations of a dwarf, to the overstrained muscles of an athlete than to the withered limbs of a weakling.

Among the tragedies, Swinburne singled out the two-part *Byron* epic as "the noblest memorial we have of its author's original powers"; among the comedies, he cited *All Fools* as "an almost faultless example of high comedy," but he reserved his most lyrical heights of praise for *The Gentleman Usher*, with its "luminous and fervent style of poetry"; and, remarkably for his time, he even appreciated the "brutal and exuberant fun" of *The Widow's Tears*. As for the poetry, Swinburne anticipated the preference of many twentieth-century critics (among them C. S. Lewis) for *Hero and Leander*, although he also found several "noble interludes of gnomic and symbolic verse" in the other minor poems. Certainly Swinburne's essay, in spite of its subjectivity, is the most perceptive as well as the fullest statement of critical opinion until modern times.[9]

In the twentieth century Chapman has had both his apologists and his detractors. Douglas Bush expressed vigorous praise in language that the Homeric translator would have appreciated: "Who touches Chapman touches a man, though an uncouth one, a brine-encrusted Odysseus over whom Athene has not shed her luminous grace."[10] C. S. Lewis,[11] on the other hand, is less kind in his wit: he objects to *The Shadow of Night*, not alone for its obscurities, but because "the passages we do understand repel us"; he condemns the moral interpolations which darkened the clarity of Homer; but for the "golden" *Banquet of Sense* he has only praise, and the continuation of *Hero and Leander* he considers the work that Chapman was really born to do.

T. S. Eliot enriched our general understanding of Chapman's poetry by linking it with the Metaphysical tradition.[12] He was among the first to recognize a close analogy between the thought and manner of Chapman and Donne: "In Chapman especially there is a direct sensuous apprehension of thought, or, a recreation of thought into feeling, which is exactly what we find in Donne." And George Williamson, in assessing the Donne tradition,[13] went so far as to label Chapman "the first Metaphysical poet." Our critical awareness of Chapman's tragedies was similarly enhanced by Ennis Rees's study of these plays[14] in terms of the main stream of Christian, humanistic drama: "[He] presented the fundamentals and subtleties of his ethical philosophy in a series of brilliant didactic tragedies. . . . He, like other Christian humanists, desired to fuse the truth of Christianity with classical wisdom."

But all this criticism—commendatory and derogatory alike, past as well as present—is to some extent fragmentary and partial: Chapman the tragedian; the translator; the metaphysical poet. The whole Chapman is missing.

II *A Contemporary View*

Not only has Chapman been fragmentized by criticism, but he has also been subjected to a few seriously mistaken interpretations which have unfortunately been perpetuated consistently through the centuries, and which have therefore hardened into pejorative labels which alienate the uninformed reader. The most central charge leveled against Chapman asserts that he was a temperamentally undramatic poet who wrote for the theater only out of necessity and who preferred to think of his plays as "poems." Nothing could be farther from the truth: Chapman had the same instinct for theatricality that marked the best of his fellow playwrights of the period. His comedies are theatrically superior to most, and quite the equal in this respect of those written by Jonson and Middleton; his tragedies are deeply rooted in the traditional homiletic structure and rich in the technique of dramaturgic contrast, much more theatrically successful than Jonson's attempts at tragedy, and compare favorably with other Jacobean pieces. In both comedy and tragedy his blank verse, functional and self-effacing, is organic to the dramatic integrity of the whole.

His plays contain a gallery of unforgettable characters: the superbly defiant Byron, the slyly hypocritical Florilla, the noble matron Cynanche, the egotistic usher Bassiolo, the vivacious diplomat M. d'Olive, and the dynamic upstart Tharsalio—to mention only a few. They also include some of the best scenes in theatrical history: Byron at his execution, vacillating between heroism and hysteria; the dying Bussy propped up by his sword;

Tharsalio dancing with glee outside the tomb; Valerio's "confession," compounded in illusion; Lodovico's hasty exit from the wrong tryst; and the drunken shipwreck at Cuckolds Haven. And they contain some of the finest dramatic verse of the period: the marriage vows of Margaret and Vincentio, the incisive cynicism of Tharsalio, the witty discourse on tobacco of M. d'Olive, and the elegiac laments of Bussy and Clermont. In characterization, action, and dialogue, Chapman proved one of the real masters of dramatic craftsmanship.

Unlike many of his contemporaries, Chapman imposed and maintained high standards for his craft. Most of his fellow playwrights, however theatrically vital, even brilliant, were on the whole fundamentally derivative, frequently mediocre, and occasionally bad. Many were willing to become hacks for businessmen like Henslowe; many descended into cynicism and crassness; most wrote hastily. But Chapman's choice of theme and technique was governed by his lofty definition of the poet's task, on stage and off; and whatever failures of clarity or effectiveness may at times be attributed to him, those of haste, superficiality, and moral indifference do not touch him.

Another popular misconception about Chapman as a dramatist is that, whatever his merits, he was not an influential force in the English drama of the time. A recent substantial study of the Jacobean stage states explicitly that Chapman was not a formative influence on the theater of that period.[15] But, again, the truth is another matter. His major historical contributions to the English stage were in comedy, where he inaugurated two significant conventions: he invented the comedy of "humours," launching it with *The Blind Beggar of Alexandria* and *A Humorous Day's Mirth;* and he initiated the romantic tragicomedy, exemplified in *The Gentleman Usher* and *Monsieur d'Olive,* which anticipate the mode adopted a decade later by Beaumont and Fletcher. One must therefore accept the judgment of T. S. Eliot, who formulated a distinction between three kinds of Elizabethan playwrights: those who would have been great even if Shakespeare had never lived, those who brought some positive contribution after Shakespeare, and those whose merit consists merely in having exploited a few Shakespearean devices. Chapman belongs in the first class.[16]

Chapman the poet has also been misjudged. The most persistent

and insidious label attached to his verse is that of obscurity. From
neo-Classic outrage over violated syntax to twentieth-century
detraction of his supposedly obfuscated style, standard criticism
has decreed Chapman an obscure poet. The fact is, however,
that obscurity as such is not apparent in most of his verse. It
is true that he sometimes wrote badly; so, in fact, do most
poets who write very much, and one may wish, as Jonson did
of Shakespeare, that Chapman had blotted out some lines.
But lapses of style are by no means equivalent to an obscure
style. Browning and Eliot, for example, are genuinely obscure
poets, for different reasons: Browning, for his involved syntax
and his logical leaps without modulation or transition; Eliot, for
his often esoteric allusiveness and his associative patterns of
thought. Chapman, in contrast, writes with exceptional clarity.
His syntax is not particularly involved although it is occasionally
incorrect. His allusions, though at times esoteric to the twentieth
century, are for the most part drawn from well-known copy-book
materials of his time. In a perceptive article on the subject, James
Smith dismisses the charge of obscurity; to him Chapman's verse
is "not only clear, but transparent: like good glass, looking
through which as a medium one is not aware of looking through
anything." [17]

Like his drama, Chapman's poetry survives on its intrinsic
merits although its total effect is more elusive and uneven than
that of his plays. The careful reader is neither befuddled by
obscurity nor piqued by "quaintness" when he encounters the
chiseled sonnets of "A Coronet to His Mistress Philosophy"; the
golden lines of the *Hero and Leander* sestiads; the fine-edged
satire in *The Tears of Peace;* and the noble albeit novel con-
ceptions of Homeric heroes in the great translations, with their
wiser and sadder Odysseus, their tragically heightened Achilles,
and their morally complicated Agamemnon. Chapman's "beyond-
sea" muse was strange but genuine. To judge him by occasional
passages of arid or topical allegory is like judging Shakespeare
on the basis of "The Phoenix and the Turtle."

Both as poet and playwright, Chapman has been traditionally
oversimplified as a static versifier and as a monolithic thinker
who did not substantially change either his literary techniques
or his views of life throughout his long career. On the contrary,
a definite but complex pattern of development, both technical

and philosophical, can be traced through his works. The subtle lyricism and delicate evocation of mood in *The Gentleman Usher* are as far from the obvious dialogue and crude plot of *The Blind Beggar of Alexandria* as Shakespeare's *Hamlet* is from *Titus Andronicus*. Chapman's developing skill is manifest. Similarly, the sophisticated stoicism of *The Tragedy of Chabot* is considerably removed from the cynical worldliness of *The Widow's Tears*, from the Platonic idealism of *Sir Giles Goosecap*, and from the Machiavellian policy of the Byron plays. These basic differences in ideational content are not merely governed by subject matter; they represent both a progression and a deepening in the author's interpretation of life.

To read Chapman is to encounter a rich and aspiring intellect, a noble and uncompromising morality, an infallible theatrical instinct, and a wavering poetic sensibility capable of separated but towering pinnacles of glorious language. To read him in the context of his time is also to meet the major themes of a paradoxical period in which the shifting complex world of Jacobean England was replacing the stable, integrated era of the Elizabethans. A final look at Chapman's central ideas, with their baroque juxtaposition of faith and skepticism, Christianity and pagan stoicism, cynicism and optimism, mysticism and naturalism, illuminates the conflicts that identify the man with his age.

III *Chapman's Philosophy*

Chapman was a learned man, "a poet that's a scholler too." He was devoted to the Classics: he loved Homer and Plutarch, absorbed Plato and Seneca, and lived by the *Enchiridion* of Epictetus. A typical Renaissance humanist, Chapman also achieved a synthesis of Classical ideas with Christianity. The streams of his Platonism and stoicism flowed into the current of his belief in basic Christian doctrine without causing turbulence.

Although few of his poems deal directly with specifically Christian themes, he appears to have been a devout man. His "Hymn to Christ the Saviour" expresses a simple, profound faith in redemption; the translations of Petrarch's penitential Psalms embody the traditional inward drama of the Christian spirit; the dramatic speech on immortality which he anachronistically places in the mouth of Cato is straightforward Christian doctrine. And in his youthful association with the freethinking Marlowe-Raleigh group of intellectuals, his name alone escaped the dangerous rumors of atheism. Basically, however, in spite of his fundamental Christian tenets, Chapman was a Platonist in his metaphysic and a stoic in his ethic.

Platonism pervades Chapman's work, although it reached him indirectly, sometimes at three removes, as in Ficino's commentary on the *Enneads* of Plotinus. Chapman accepted Plato's metaphysical idealism, and an awareness of the analogous planes of spirit and matter, reality and illusion, underlies almost his every word. He assumed a correspondence between these two planes, viewing the phenomenal world as an imperfect copy of the ideal realm. He also accepted Plato's moral dualism, and the code of virtue implicit in all of his writings emphasizes the welfare of the soul over that of the body.

In his view of learning Chapman adopted the Platonic equation of wisdom and virtue, and he idealized the scholar as the supremely good man. His comedies all place the portrait of a genuine scholar in juxtaposition with that of a mere pedant, and his tragedies expose the villainy of ignorance while defining the tragic flaw of the hero as a fault in his learning. He also adhered to the Platonic theory of the intuitive knowledge of the soul together with its correlate theory of recollection. Apparent obscurities in the plays and in such a poem as *The Shadow of Night* can often be traced to an esoteric Platonic or Plotinian source which expresses this elusive doctrine.

Chapman paid repeated homage to the Platonic ladder of love. The most explicit example is *Ovid's Banquet* in which the hero rises by degrees from sensible to intellective love, but hierarchical distinctions on the ladder of love are also the concern of many of the plays. His portraits of women run the gamut of possibility from the idealized matron Cynanche, to the corrupt and faithless wife Cynthia. Similarly, his men in love range from the scholarly Clarence, who is spiritually smitten with his intellectual equal, Eugenia, to the cynical Tharsalio, who confirms his conviction that no woman can transcend her native sensuality. The bachelor playwright proved a skilled theorist of love.

In addition to these basic doctrines, several images from the Platonic dialogues occur in the plays and poems of Chapman. For instance the metamorphosis of a soul into a star, an idea from the *Timaeus,* occurs repeatedly. Bussy's fiery soul is on its way to becoming a star at the conclusion of that tragedy as is that of Byron in the last act of his epic drama.

But Chapman was more of a moralist than a philosopher. The expression of his stoical ethic achieves both greater clarity and more frequent emphasis than that of his Platonic ideas. His stoic ideal is forcefully stated in his poetry and exemplified in his plays. His stoic mentors were Epictetus, with whom he seems to have had a particular intellectual and temperamental affinity, and those Renaissance favorites, Plutarch, Seneca, and Cicero. Not only were several of Chapman's characters modeled on the stoic ideal but many dramatic speeches are also close paraphrases of their sources in stoic writings.

The central stoical idea reflected in the works of Chapman is the superiority of inner tranquillity over outward achievement. Several of his dramatic heroes achieve success or failure in life in terms of this standard. An outstanding exemplar of the victory of inner fortitude over outward affliction is the secondary figure of Strozza in *The Gentleman Usher,* who recuperates from a symbolic wound: the arrow drops out of his flesh at the moment he prophesies because of his stoic conviction. He strikingly illustrates that the spiritual peace which can triumph over the perturbations of the flesh involves not merely passive acceptance of destiny but an active establishment of harmony with it. The stoic hero does not rebel against or contend with his lot; he resolves to want whatever it is his lot to have. Two tragic heroes who embody this ideal are Clermont, so perfectly stoic that he needs to be prodded by the vindictive ghost of his brother to carry out the duty of vengeance, and Chabot, who is so sublimely innocent of the crime he is convicted of that he dies broken-hearted because he received a pardon for it. The failure of the stoic ideal is illustrated in the passionate, impetuous figures of Bussy and Byron, who, in rebelling against their fate, become victims of it.

The unifying theme of Chapman's eclectic philosophy is dualism. His dualistic view of man assumed both vertical and horizontal forms. Vertical dualism, the ascendancy of spirit over flesh, predicates a hierarchical vision of reality. Man, midway on "the chain of being," may transcend the flesh to soar into the realm of Plotinian pure spirit, of the stoic logos, of heavenly wisdom. Chapman thus exalts man's aspiring intellect. Horizontal dualism, on the other hand, involves the supremacy of the inward

self over outward circumstances. Man may endure external bondage if his intellect is free; he is fortified against physical suffering
by inward wisdom; he can resist the distractions of the outer
world by concentrating on the divine spark of illumination within
his soul. All of Chapman's poetry is dedicated to the upward and
the inward; it is also committed to the search for higher and
deeper reality.

IV *Epilogue*

In Alfred Noyes' verse *Tales of the Mermaid Tavern*, George
Chapman appears as a character in the episode called "The Sign
of the Golden Shoe." The description of the poet's physiognomy
fancifully captures the Classic components of his thought:

> Chapman, with something of the steady strength
> That helms our ships, and something of the Greek,
> The cool clear passion of Platonic thought
> Behind the fringe of his Olympian beard
> And broad Homeric brows, confront[ed] him
> Gravely.

Notes and References

CHAPTER ONE

1. *Thomas Nashe*, ed. Stanley Wells (London, 1964). In "Terrors of the Night," p. 172.

2. For biographical details see the following articles: Mark Eccles, "Chapman's Early Years," *Studies in Philology*, XLIII (1946), 176–193; Jean Robertson, "Early Life of George Chapman," *Modern Language Review*, XL (1945), 157–65; C. J. Sisson and Robert Butman, "George Chapman, 1612–22: Some New Facts," *Modern Language Review*, XLVI (1951), 185–90.

3. William Rowley and John Webster, *Cure for a Cuckold*, II, i, in *The Complete Works of John Webster*, ed. F. L. Lucas (London, 1927), Vol. III.

4. In *Athenae Oxonienses* (London, 1721), I, 591–93.

5. Muriel Bradbrook, *The School of Night: A Study in the Literary Relationships of Sir Walter Raleigh* (Cambridge, 1936). Miss Bradbrook postulated a definite "school." Recent opinion assumes a considerably less formal relationship among these bright young men.

6. A manuscript collection containing copies of several letters signed by George Chapman and others attributed to him is on repository in the Folger Shakespeare Library. Edited by Bertram Dobell, most of the letters appeared serially in the 1901 volume of the *Athenaeum*, with commentary by the editor.

7. For a description of the distinct styles of entertainment offered by the public and the private theaters, see Alfred Harbage, *Shakespeare and the Rival Traditions* (New York, 1952).

8. From the letter of the French ambassador, La Boderie, quoted in English translation in Parrott's edition of the tragedies.

9. The theory that the play is based on an actual historical situation is advanced by Norma Dobie Solve, *Stuart Politics in Chapman's Tragedy of Chabot* (Ann Arbor, 1928).

10. See below, Chapter six.

11. See the letter quoted on p. 29.

12. Inigo Jones, the architect who designed sets for many of Jonson's

masques, also prepared the pageant for *The Masque of the Inner Temple.*

13. See Allardyce Nicoll, "The Dramatic Portrait of George Chapman," *Philological Quarterly,* XLI (1962), 215–28.

14. This epigram, "On Learning," was published with other translations in the volume entitled *Petrarchs Seven Penitential Psalms, with Other Philosophical Poems,* and is included in Bartlett's edition of the complete poems of Chapman.

CHAPTER TWO

1. *The Dialogues of Plato,* trans. Benjamin Jowett (Oxford, 4th ed., 1953).

2. George Puttenham, *The Arte of English Poesie,* Book III, ch. 3. In *Elizabethan Critical Essays,* ed. G. Gregory Smith (Oxford, 1904), Vol. II.

3. Benedetto Croce and others have noted Donne's "felt thought."

4. T. S. Eliot, "The Metaphysical Poets," in *Selected Essays, 1917–1932* (New York, 1932), pp. 241–50.

5. George Williamson, *The Donne Tradition* (Cambridge, Mass.: 1930).

6. The dates of Donne's poems are uncertain as they were apparently circulated in manuscript long before published.

7. Douglas Bush has pointed out that the most likely source of the five-fold vision which constitutes the argument of the poem is Ficino's discussion of Ratio, Visus, Auditus, Olfactus, Gustus, and Tactus in his Commentary on the Convivium. See Bush, *Mythology and the Renaissance Tradition* (rev. ed.; New York, 1963).

8. "The Philosopher saith, Intellectus in ipsa intelligibilia transit, upon which is grounded thys inuention, that in the same manner his life might passe into hys Mistres conceite, which by this Analogie, should bee *Intellectus,* & her conceit, *Intelligibilis.*"

9. C. S. Lewis, *English Literature in the Sixteenth Century* (Oxford, 1954), pp. 513–14.

10. F. L. Schoell, *Etudes sur l'humanisme continental en Angleterre.* (Paris, 1926).

11. For example, from one of his sonnets:

> I am gall, I am heartburn. God's most deep decree
> Bitter would have me taste: my taste was me;
> Bones built in me, flesh filled, blood brimmed the curse.
> Selfyeast of spirit a dull dough sours. . . .

12. Philip Sidney, "Apologie for Poetry," in Smith, *op. cit.*

13. Echoing Chapman, Daniel has Musophilus say, "This is the thing that I was born to do . . ." (l. 577).

14. Although much modern literature is allegorical (e.g., *The Plague*

by Albert Camus and *The Trial* by Franz Kafka), the word has become generally pejorative.

15. Like all practicing playwrights of his time, he habitually looked for new variations on popular old conventions. The same practice was followed by the sonneteers.

16. Even Roy W. Battenhouse, whose scholarly article ("Chapman's The Shadow of Night: An Interpretation," *Studies in Philology,* XXXVIII [1941], 584–608) is excellent, specifies that the Panther is Pride and the Boar is Lust, but the more general symbolism of the beasts as embodiments of the sins of spirit and flesh seems more fitting to the poem.

17. For a summary of the elegy see F. L. Schoell, "George Chapman and the Italian Neo-Latinists of the Quattrocento," *Modern Philology,* XIII (1915), 23–46.

18. Theo. As if that could applied be to a Man?
    O barraine Malice! was it euer sayd
    A man was barraine? or the burthen layd
    Of bearing fruite on Man? if not, nor this
    Epithete barraine, can be construed his
    In least proprietie. (ll. 122–28)

19. Bush, *op. cit.*, p. 200.

20. Matthew Arnold, "On Translating Homer," Lecture I, in *Arnold's Essays in Criticism* (Oxford, 1914).

21. *Ibid.*

22. George de Forest Lord, *Homeric Renaissance* (New Haven, 1956), *passim.*

23. Yeats resembles Chapman in his concern with "perning in the gyre," flux in contrast with permanence, perhaps attainable only in art.

24. Allardyce Nicoll, *Chapman's Homer* (New York, 1956), p. 501.

25. See Phyllis Bartlett, ed. *The Poems of George Chapman* (New York, 1941).

CHAPTER THREE

1. For example, W. Macneile Dixon writes in the *Cambridge History of English Literature* (Cambridge University Press, 1932): "He was a poet; but his muse did not point him toward the theatre" (VI, 33).

2. "Induction" to *Every Man in His Humour.*

3. See Ennis Rees, "Chapman's *Blind Beggar* and the Marlovian Hero," *Journal of English and Germanic Philology,* LVII (1958), 60–63.

4. Cf. Hamlet's lament about the world as "an unweeded garden." Both speeches reflect the *contemptus mundi* theme.

5. A parody of the following passage in *Euphues:* "As therefore

the sweetest rose hath his prickle, the finest velvet his brack, the fairest flour his bran." In John Lyly, *Works*, ed. R. W. Bond (Oxford, 1902), I, 84.

6. Cf. Shakespeare's conversion of courtesans into wives in *A Comedy of Errors*.

7. For example, Sir Fopling Flutter in *The Man of Mode* by George Etheredge.

8. Cf. *Love's Labour's Lost*.

9. Modern commentators are in general agreement with this judgment.

10. The *commedia erudita* turned to Classic models, unlike the *commedia dell arte* which resorted to improvisation and the native tradition.

11. See Parrott's remarks in his edition of the *Comedies*.

12. *Ibid.*, p. 896.

CHAPTER FOUR

1. For further discussion of the nature of tragicomedy, see Cyrus Hoy, *The Hyacinth Room* (New York, 1964) and F. H. Ristine, *English Tragi-Comedy* (New York, 1910).

2. The mutilation theme occurs in Book I where Parthenia is attacked by a rejected suitor who smears her face with poison. Her beauty is subsequently restored by a physician.

3. In the *Heptameron* (Nov. 10) the chaste Florinda bruises her face with a stone in order to protect her threatened honor. This tale is borrowed by both Pettie and Painter.

4. . . . yet Adelasia,
   In Pettie's *Palace of Pleasure*,
   For all the world, with such a knife as thus
   Cut off her cheeks and nose, and was commended

More than all dames that kept their faces whole. (V, iii, 32–36) Chapman's memory of the stories was confused: not only is the title inaccurate, but also elements of the Florinda and Parthenia plots are intermingled.

5. The rivalry between Raleigh's circle and that of Essex (including Shakespeare) involved the controversy between the artist, favored by the intellectual, formally educated Raleigh group, and the villanist, exemplified by such inspired but untutored geniuses as Shakespeare.

6. A fact which would identify him, in the Renaissance scheme of things, as a symbol of moral chaos.

7. In his Introduction to his edition of *The Gentleman Usher and All Fools* (Boston, 1907), p. xliii.

8. See Henry Weidner, "The Dramatic Uses of Homeric Idealism: The Significance of Theme and Design in George Chapman's *The*

Gentleman Usher," English Literary History, XXVIII (1961), 121–26.

9. The anonymous tragedy entitled *Charlemagne* was for a long time attributed to Chapman, partly on the basis of this theme; but scholars have now rejected his authorship. In his edition of the plays, Parrott disclaims it as the work of Chapman.

10. Petrarch's *Colloquium de Contemptu Mundi* was popularly known as *Secretum.* Written about 1342, it takes the form of a dialogue between the Renaissance poet and the early Christian philosopher St. Augustine.

11. *The Tragedy of Chabot* was ostensibly written in collaboration with Shirley although Shirley's contributions are slight and consist of added scenes. See Chapter six.

12. Alfred Noyes has written a second farewell for Greene in his dramatic narrative, *Tales of the Mermaid Tavern* (New York, [ca. 1913]).

13. Algernon Swinburne, "George Chapman" in *The Complete Works,* ed. Sir Edmund Gosse and Thomas Wise. (London, 1875), XII, 172.

14. Thomas More, *Utopia,* ed. J. Churton Collins (Oxford, 1904), p. 78.

15. According to one of Chapman's letters in the Dobell Collection (*op. cit.*), Marston escaped imprisonment.

16. Parrott, *The Comedies,* II, 848.

17. Tharsalio remarks, "Well, out of this perhaps there may be moulded matter of more mirth than my baffling" (I, iii, 133–34). *The Widow's Tears,* like the other plays discussed in this chapter, manifests rather the reverse: more matter than mirth.

18. Petronius' *Satyricon* is the primary but not exclusive source of this play. Chapman apparently follows an earlier version than Petronius in having the husband himself try the virtue of his supposed widow.

19. The figure of the Governor is a throwback not only to the morality Vice, with whom he is explicitly identified, but to the whole medieval tradition of ritual perversion, exemplified in the Lord of Misrule, the Festa Asinorum. ("The Governor will have asses bear good qualities, and wise men shall use them.")

20. *Virtù* is a significant, complex word in the Renaissance. In its popular Machiavellian usage, it referred to a wholly amoral, individualistic self-aggrandizement; some writers, however, tried to unite external *Virtù* with internal *Virtue* in an idealized hero. Chapman's heroes all possess *Virtù* but vary according to their *Virtue.*

CHAPTER FIVE

1. Ennis Rees, *The Tragedies of George Chapman* (Cambridge, Mass., 1954), pp. 30–31, 51–52, and *passim.*

2. See the chapter on "Freedom and Necessity" in Ernst Cassirer, *The Individual and the Cosmos in Renaissance Philosophy*, trans. Mario Domandi (New York, 1963), p. 96.

3. See the statements of Dryden quoted in Chapter Seven.

4. From Donne's "An Anatomy of the World: First Anniversarie," l. 213.

5. See the following different interpretations of Bussy: C. L. Barber, "The Ambivalence of Bussy D'Ambois," *Review of English Literature*, II (1961), 38–44; Michael Higgins, "Chapman's 'Senecal Man': A Study in Jacobean Psychology," *Review of English Studies*, XXI (1945), 183–91; Michael Higgins, "The Development of the 'Senecal Man': Chapman's Bussy D'Ambois and Some Precursors," *Review of English Studies*, XXIII (1947), 24–33; Edwin Muir, "Royal Man: Notes on the Tragedies of George Chapman," *Essays on Literature and Society* (London, 1949), pp. 20–30; R. H. Perkinson, "Nature and the Tragic Hero in Chapman's Bussy Plays," *Modern Language Quarterly*, III (1942), 263–85; Irving Ribner, "Character and Theme in Chapman's Bussy D'Ambois," *English Literary History*, XXVI (1959), 482–96; Eugene Waith, *The Herculean Hero: In Marlowe, Chapman, Shakespeare, and Dryden* (New York, 1962), pp. 88–111.

6. Eliot's phrase occurs in his essay "Hamlet and His Problems," *op. cit.*, pp. 121–26.

7. See the discussion of the conflict between greatness and goodness in Rees, *op. cit.*, p. 160 and *passim.*

8. See Parrott, *The Tragedies*, II, p. 591.

9. For a discussion of Machiavellianism in Chapman see Robert Ornstein, *The Moral Vision of Jacobean Tragedy* (Madison, 1960), pp. 47–83.

10. See Johnstone Parr, "The Duke of Byron's Malignant Caput Algol," *Studies in Philology*, XLIII (1946), 194–202.

11. The man of "policy" is to Chapman (as to most of his contemporary playwrights) an evil figure, a blind self-seeker and a natural enemy of virtue and justice.

CHAPTER SIX

1. Andrew Marvell's poem "The Garden" offers a contemporary analogue:

> The mind, that ocean where each kind
> Does straight its own resemblance find;
> Yet it creates, transcending these,

> Far other worlds and other seas,
> Annihilating all that's made
> To a green thought in a green shade.

2. The enormous popularity of the revenge formula led playwrights to seek ever new variations on the old formula.

3. See Parrott, *The Tragedies*, II, 632–33.

4. See Emil Koeppel, *Quellen-Studien zu den Dramen George Chapman's, Philip Massinger's and John Ford's* (Strassburg, 1897).

5. Norma Dobie Solve, *Stuart Politics in Chapman's 'Tragedy of Chabot'* (Ann Arbor, 1928), is devoted entirely to proving this hypothesis.

6. For a discussion of the parallel trial scenes, see Irving Ribner, "The Meaning of Chapman's Tragedy of Chabot," *Modern Language Review*, LV (1960), 321–31.

7. See Elias Schwarz, "A Neglected Play by Chapman," *Studies in Philology*, LVIII (1960), 140–59.

8. See Peter Ure, "Chapman's Tragedies," *Jacobean Theatre* ("Stratford-upon-Avon Studies No. 1," [London, 1960]), pp. 227–47.

9. See Parrott, *The Tragedies*, II, 655.

10. See Ennis Rees, *op. cit.*, pp. 126–55; J. E. Ingledew, "The Date of Composition of Chapman's Caesar and Pompey," *Review of English Studies*, XII (1936), 144–59; Elias Schwarz, "The Dates and Order of Chapman's Tragedies," *Modern Philology*, LVII (1959), 80–82.

CHAPTER SEVEN

1. In *Palladis Tamia*, originally published in 1598.

2. Included in John Dryden, *Dramatic Essays* (London, 1931), p. 157.

3. *Ibid.*, "Examen Poeticum," p. 206.

4. Charles Lamb, *Specimens of English Dramatic Poets*, ed. William Mac Donald (London, 1921), I, 198.

5. "The Revolt of Islam" is prefaced by the following epitaph: "There is no danger to a man that knows / What life and death is: There's not any law / Exceeds his knowledge; neither is it lawful / That he should stoop to any other law."

6. Arnold, *op. cit.*, p. 263.

7. Swinburne, *op. cit.*

8. The sonnet is as follows:

> High priest of Homer, not elect in vain,
>> Deep trumpets blow before thee, shawns behind
>> Mix music with the rolling wheels that wind
> Slow through the labouring triumph of thy train:
> Fierce history, molten in thy forging brain,
>> Takes form and fire and fashion from thy mind,

Tormented and transmuted out of kind:
But howsoe'er thou shift thy strenuous strain,
Like Tailor smooth, like Fisher swollen, and now
    Grim Yarrington scarce bloodier marked than thou,
    Then bluff as Mayne's or broad-mouthed Barry's glee;
Proud still with hoar predominance of brow
    And beard like foam swept off the broad blown sea,
    Where'er thou go, men's reverence goes with thee.

9. The only general, full-length studies of Chapman in the twentieth century were written in French, Italian, and German: Jean Jacquot, *George Chapman* (Paris, 1951); Marcello Pagnini, *Forme e Motivi nella Poesie e nelle Tragedie di George Chapman* (Firenze, 1957); Nancy von Pogrell, *Die philosophisch-poètische Entwicklung George Chapmans* (Hamburg, 1939).

10. Bush, *op. cit.*, p. 200.

11. Lewis, *op. cit.*, p. 511.

12. "The Metaphysical Poets."

13. Williamson, *op. cit.*, pp. 58–59.

14. Rees, *op. cit.*, p. 1.

15. Ornstein, *op. cit.*, pp. 47–83.

16. Eliot, "The Elizabethan Dramatists," *op. cit.*, pp. 91–99.

17. Smith, *op. cit.*, p. 345.

Selected Bibliography

PRIMARY SOURCES

Chapman's Homer. Ed. Allardyce Nicoll. New York: Pantheon Books, 1956. 2 vols.

Homer's Batrachomiomachia and Other Translations by George Chapman. Ed. Richard Hooper. London: J. R. Smith, 1858. (Includes the *Georgics* of Hesiod, the *Hero and Leander* of Musaeus, and the *Fifth Satire* of Juvenal.)

The Comedies of George Chapman. Ed. Thomas Marc Parrott. London: Routledge and Kegan Paul, Ltd., 1913. (Also includes *The Ball*, formerly and mistakenly attributed to Chapman.)

The Poems of George Chapman. Ed. Phyllis Bartlett. New York: Modern Language Association, 1941.

The Tragedies of George Chapman. Ed. Thomas Marc Parrott. London: Routledge and Kegan Paul, Ltd., 1910. (Also includes *Alphonsus* and *Revenge for Honour*, formerly and mistakenly attributed to Chapman.)

SECONDARY SOURCES

BARTLETT, PHYLLIS B. "The Heroes of Chapman's Homer," *Review of English Studies*, XVII (1941), 257–80. A perspective on the heroes of the *Iliad* as Platonic; of the *Odyssey*, as Stoic.

BATTENHOUSE, RAY. "Chapman's 'Shadow of Night': An Interpretation," *Studies in Philology*, XXXVIII (1941), 584–608. Erudite, detailed analysis of Chapman's most difficult poem.

———. "Chapman and the Nature of Man," *English Literary History*, XII (1945), 87–107. An interpretation from the viewpoint of four myths: Ganymede, Prometheus, Hercules, the Senecal man.

CASSIRER, ERNST. *The Individual and the Cosmos in Renaissance Philosophy.* Trans. Mario Domandi. New York: Harper and Row, 1963. This valuable study illuminates the philosophical background of Chapman's theme of learning.

JACQUOT, JEAN. *George Chapman, 1559–1634, sa vie, sa poèsie, son theatre, sa pensée.* Paris: Annales de l'Université de Lyon, 1951. Sound, comprehensive study.

171

KENNEDY, C. W. "Political Theory in the Plays of George Chapman" in *Essays in Dramatic Literature: The Parrott Presentation Volume*. Ed. Hardin Craig. Princeton: Princeton University Press, 1935. Careful study of major tragic theme of political justice.

KRISTELLER, P. O. *The Philosophy of Marsilio Ficino*. Trans. Virginia Conant. New York: Columbia University Press, 1943. Important background for understanding Chapman's use of Platonic doctrine.

LORD, GEORGE DE FOREST. *Homeric Renaissance: the Odyssey of George Chapman*. New Haven: Yale University Press, 1956. Excellent critical and historical evaluation of the *Odyssey* translation.

NICOLL, ALLARDYCE. "The Dramatic Portrait of George Chapman," *Philological Quarterly*, XLI (1962), 215–28. A lively account of the Bellamont figure in *Northward Ho* as a portrait of Chapman.

PERKINSON, R. H. "Nature and the Tragic Hero in Chapman's Bussy Plays," *Modern Language Quarterly*, III (1942), 263–85. A consideration of the culpable role of nature in the tragedies.

REES, ENNIS. *The Tragedies of George Chapman*. Cambridge. Mass.: Harvard University Press, 1954. Excellent study of the tragedies in terms of their Christian humanism.

SCHOENBAUM, SAMUEL. "The Widows Tears and the Other Chapman," *Huntington Library Quarterly*, XXIII (1960), 321–38. A useful consideration of the comic and satiric side of the playwright.

SCHWARZ, ELIAS. "A Neglected Play by Chapman," *Studies in Philology*, LVIII (1956), 140–59. A defense of the unity of conception and characterization in *Caesar and Pompey*.

SMITH, JAMES. "George Chapman," *Scrutiny*, III (1934–35), 339–50; IV (1935–36), 45–61. Perceptive, unconventional interpretation of the poet and dramatist.

SOLVE, NORMA DOBIE. *Stuart Politics in Chapman's Tragedy of Chabot*. Ann Arbor: University of Michigan, 1928. Convincing case for the analogy between the Chabot plot and the successive trials of Somerset and Bacon.

SWINBURNE, ALGERNON. "George Chapman" in *The Complete Works*, XII, 136–251. Eds. Sir Edmund Gosse and Thomas Wise. London: William Heineman, Ltd., 1875. Sympathetic but by no means adulatory study; classic in its critical perceptions, written in highly metaphorical style.

URE, PETER. "Chapman as Translator and Tragic Playwright," *Guide to English Literature*, II, 318–33. Baltimore: Penguin Books, 1963. Effective essay; offers original insights.

WEIDNER, HENRY. "The Dramatic Uses of Homeric Idealism: The Significance of Theme and Design in George Chapman's 'The Gentleman Usher,'" *English Literary History*, XXVIII (1961),

121–36. A ritualistic interpretation of the play which analyzes plot structure in terms of ceremonies and anti-ceremonies.

WIELER, JOHN WILLIAM. *George Chapman—The Effect of Stoicism upon His Tragedies.* New York: King's Crown Press, 1949. Limited but the only full-length study of this important subject.

WILLIAMSON, GEORGE. *The Donne Tradition.* Cambridge, Mass.: Harvard University Press, 1930. The only consideration of Chapman as a metaphysical poet.

Index

175